Penguin Education

Second-Language Learning
Myth and Reality

Paul Christophersen

Penguin Modern Linguistic Texts

General Editor

David Crystal

Advisory Board

Dwight Bolinger
M. A. K. Halliday
John Lyons
Frank Palmer
James Sledd
C. I. J. M. Stuart

Paul Christophersen

Second-Language Learning
Learning
Myth and Reality

Penguin Education

Penguin Education
A Division of Penguin Books Ltd,
Harmondsworth, Middlesex, England
Penguin Books Inc, 7110 Ambassador Road,
Baltimore, Md 21207, USA
Penguin Books Australia Ltd,
Ringwood, Victoria, Australia

First published 1973
Copyright © Paul Christophersen, 1973

Made and printed in Great Britain by
Cox & Wyman Ltd,
London, Reading and Fakenham
Set in Monotype Times

Acknowledgements

I am indebted to Dr A. W. H. Buffery of the University of Oxford for advice and suggestions regarding the argument presented in section 18. The information about exotic and East European languages on pages 38–9 comes in part from Professors K. Bergsland, A. Gallis and H. Henne of the University of Oslo. While recording my thanks to these helpers, I absolve them from any blame for faulty digestion on my part.

Contents

Four Bilingualism

Five Planning

One The State of the Art

1 Myth and realism

From earliest times we find in man's attitude to his language a curious mixture of myth and realism, of supernatural belief and scientific observation. Almost jostling each other in time are legends like the Tower of Babel and attempts at systematic description like the work of the early Sanskrit grammarians. An experiment with language learning carried out under the Pharaoh Psammetichus (see section 14) was largely scientific in conception, and yet it rested on an unconfirmed belief in the hereditary nature of language, probably linked with a religious belief.

This mixture of myth and realism has continued throughout the ages, even though the proportions may have changed. The development of a truly scientific attitude to language belongs largely to the nineteenth and twentieth centuries of our era. During that period our methods of investigation in both the historical and contemporary fields have grown in consistency and precision. Nevertheless, despite the prevailing scientific attitude there are probably still, as this book will contend (see especially chapters 3 and 4), areas of our thinking about language, and about language learning in particular, in which not only laymen but linguists are prone to mysticism and myth making, or at least to an undue degree of subjectivity.

2 Ideas about language learning

Language teaching and language learning are fields of activity which are engaging a great and growing amount of human attention and energy. Thousands upon thousands of people make a living by teaching languages, and millions of others spend scores of man-hours each, trying to learn. Every year large numbers of books and articles appear dealing with language instruction in all its aspects. Some publishers derive a considerable part of their income from the sale of language courses, and other firms specialize in making teaching aids. Language instruction occupies a fair proportion of broadcasting time in many countries, and television companies are beginning to catch up. There is every reason to think that all these activities will go on increasing in volume and intensity for a long time to come.

In view of the time and energy expended on this subject, it is natural to ask if the matter is being approached in the right manner, in accordance with the best available knowledge. The present writer has misgivings on this point. We are uncertain, many of us, not only about methods of instruction but about aims – partly, no doubt, because we have an insufficiently clear notion of what the different aims involve to enable us to make a choice between them. There is a great deal of talk about the need for improvement in second-language teaching: but suppose we are really successful, suppose we found a way of making it possible in a relatively short space of time to train an Italian to use English in speech and writing like an Englishman, would that please us? Would we welcome it as the answer to our hopes and prayers, or would we hate the new picture that presented itself of a world in which national identity was no longer a simple and clear-cut matter?

Some people would dismiss these speculations as unrealistic. An elaborate mythology has grown up, as Sapon (1965, pp. 132–3) says,

of what is possible and what is impossible for humans to learn with respect to second languages. The arguments to justify these myths run the full range from sociocultural explanations to neurophysiological suggestions that after the age of ten a kind of neuromuscular rigidity and cortical hardening begins increasingly to impede the acquisition of bilingual behaviour. Exceptions – that do not *prove* but *test* the rule – are explained as cases of infantilism, or more generously as the result of rare personality factors or motivational states.

Others take a different view. A few years ago, in discussing programmed teaching, Carroll (1963, pp. 138–9) threw out a hint that language teaching might conceivably become over-efficient:

If it regularly produced students with perfect native accents, startling fluency in speaking, high proficiency in reading and writing, and decided empathy for a foreign culture, one can realize the educational pandemonium that might result. The educational system might not be able to absorb such students, or they might to some extent be less acceptable in a foreign country than if they exhibited a suitably non-native accent.

In fact, the nature of language learning is such that no sudden breakthrough like this is likely to happen; but gradual approximations will occur, and even under present conditions complete success, whether or not we choose to call it exceptional, is by no means impossible. Do we, when it comes to the point, want to aim at perfection? If not, how do we ensure that learning stops short at just the right point? Because, after all, teaching human beings is not like filling bottles.

3 The position of linguistics

The picture of language teaching that has just been presented may strike some as unduly optimistic. Can we in fact hope to improve our methods? Considering 'the state of the art', is there ever likely to be any noticeable improvement? The would-be learner nowadays is faced with a bewildering variety of competing methods, a veritable *embarras de richesse*: the Phonetic Method, the Structural Method, the Nature Method, the Eclectic Method, etc. How is he to choose? The language teacher is in the same situation, or a worse one it might seem, because he is professionally involved and will consider it his duty to be well informed. But from whom is he to seek advice? Can linguistic theory help? If he consults the professional journals, he will be faced with an array of conflicting opinions. He is likely to be told by one writer (e.g. Ritchie, 1967) that generative grammar has implications for foreign-language courses, and by another (e.g. Lamendella, 1969) that it is a complete failure in language teaching. He will be told by one authority (e.g. Jakobovits, 1968) that pattern drills are without theoretical foundation in the latest orthodoxy, and by another (e.g. Brown, 1969) that they are indispensable and in fact not opposed to transformational or any other kind of grammar. He will find a writer like Roddis (1968) discovering to his surprise that 'many of the theories and techniques which currently attract epithets such as "new" or "revolutionary" in fact owe their genesis to writers such as Sweet, Jespersen, or Palmer, each writing over half a century ago' (see also p. 17). And he will find the same writer equally surprised at the frequent unanimity among those early reformers, because – sad to relate – this is no longer the case among those discussing language teaching today.

In one sense this situation is by no means new. In 1899 Henry Sweet observed somewhat sourly (1899, p. viii): 'until every one recognizes that there is no royal road to languages ... the public will continue to run after one new method after the other, only to return disappointed to the old routine'. And further on (p. 86) he asserted that 'nothing will ever make the learning of languages easy'. Sixty-five years later Halliday, McIntosh and Strevens (1964, pp. viii–ix) had to admit that traditional language teaching in its various forms has usually 'succeeded in attaining at least its main objectives', and as regards improvement a complicating factor is that 'there is not in operation, except in the vaguest sense, any generally current and accepted body of theory, or system of practice'. The chief difference since the late nineteenth century appears to be that nowadays it is not just the public but professional linguists who keep running after new methods and techniques – or old ones under new names.

Some people have pinned their faith on 'hardware'. First it was the gramophone and later the tape-recorder and then the language laboratory. There were even those at one time who predicted that the machine might eventually replace the teacher. After a period of extravagant enthusiasm in some quarters it seems now pretty clear that nothing of the kind will happen. Technological development, such as radio, films and television as well as easier and cheaper travel, has indeed made a difference, a great difference. It has made spoken contact with foreigners in their own language a likely part of the average person's experience. As such it is an extremely important aid, but it has made no difference to the theory of language learning.

Why has linguistics failed us in this way? Why have linguists not been able to any appreciable extent to ease the task of the learner, or at least to guide him with more success? Linguistics, being the science of language, ought, it would seem, to have something of importance to say in a matter of this kind. One difficulty is in a sense self-imposed. Many linguists nowadays regard the analysis of linguistic structure as their central and perhaps their only concern; but we cannot assume axiomatically, as linguists are inclined to do – or were in the 1950s and 1960s – that the units used in analysing language are also those needed in learning it. The learning process is clearly a psychological one, and psychology until recently was not part of the linguist's concern. It was with this in mind that Mackey a few years ago (1966, p. 199) said that 'if the linguist claims that such and such a method is the best way to learn the language, he is speaking outside his competence.'

In recent years the horizon has indeed widened, and a great deal of work has been done in the border areas between linguistics and other disciplines relevant to language learning (Lyons, 1970) such as sociology, psychology and neurology. We still know all too little in some of these areas; but there is probably a greater realization now than a couple of decades ago of the limits of our knowledge, and the earlier unshakable faith in 'all-inclusive magico-scientific solutions' (Ferguson, 1971, p. 4) to the problem of language learning has partly – but only partly – given way to a more realistic appraisal. The present volume will take up certain points concerning language learning where our outlook is still unrealistic, 'mythical' rather than scientific. It will argue that there is not in theory any limit to the degree of proficiency that may be achieved in a second language, and that consequently the traditional distinction between 'native' and 'non-native' in language is of doubtful validity. And, since successful language learning leads to bilingualism, a state of affairs fraught with many difficulties, a consideration of these problems will take up a substantial part of this book. But before we enter upon these discussions it will be necessary to review very briefly some of the more important ideas on language learning that have been held by linguists and others.

Two Some Linguistic, Psychological and Other Views on Language Learning

4 The beginnings

When did linguists begin to take an active interest in language learning? Two quite distinct answers to this question are likely to be given by different people, depending on the length of their perspective. Some, like Haugen (1955), say 'in the 1880s and 1890s'; others, like DeCamp (1969), say 'after the Second World War'. In fact, as has often been pointed out, interesting and sound ideas about language learning can be traced back a very long way, to Comenius, for example; but a more professional approach had to wait upon the development of linguistics and related sciences in the second half of the nineteenth century; and it was not till after 1945 that language teachers in America began to take serious notice of linguistics.

The leading figures in the nineteenth-century Reform Movement were Sweet (1877, 1889), Viëtor (1882), Franke (1884), Passy and Jespersen (1904). It is a matter of some significance that these people were all phoneticians. It must have seemed to them that the problem of pronunciation in foreign-language teaching had been solved once and for all with the development of phonetics, because with the help of this body of knowledge a good or even a perfect accent was no longer an unattainable ideal for the foreign learner. Certainly it seemed to Jespersen, with whom the present writer was personally acquainted, that the main problem in language learning after the initial stage was not that of learning ordinary everyday speech, but of acquiring a 'native-like' feeling for the language, especially in matters of literary style (Christophersen, 1972).

This is a point that deserves to be emphasized, because there is reason to think that the traditional distinction between 'native' and 'foreign', which this book will attempt to invalidate, is in some way linked with the common observation that foreigners usually speak with a marked accent. There is evidence to suggest that some exotic communities do not possess the concept 'foreign accent' and consequently do not distinguish between 'native' and 'non-native' speakers, much to the embarrassment of visitors with only a slight knowledge of the language (Hill, 1970). While in our western societies some people might be prepared to concede that, under favourable conditions, a foreigner could conceivably achieve indistinguishability in the writing of their language, they are usually convinced that something prevents him from ever achieving the same in speech, something which was decided irrevocably in the first few years of his life. If the thesis of this book is correct, the development of phonetics could be claimed with some justice to be the greatest, and perhaps the only major, advance in language teaching in the course of human history.

What adherents of the Reform Movement advocated has sometimes been referred to as the Direct Method (Passy's term), but it is in fact less of a method than a general approach. They wanted to introduce the results of phonetic science into language teaching. They advocated the importance of the living language, of teaching speech. And they wanted to adopt the psychological principles of association and of visualization and learning through the senses, for instance by means of pictures and through play and activity. They emphasized the importance of learning grammar by practice rather than precept, by making the responses to points of grammar automatic. Altogether they wanted as close an approximation as possible to the way a small child learns his first language; the mother tongue should be avoided as much as possible and translation reduced to a minimum. They held that learning a language in this way meant the absorption of another culture, another way of life and another outlook.

One reason for giving this long list of ideas is to show that the Direct Method does not – or not necessarily – mean 'total immersion', a term which has sometimes been used to describe it, often with unfavourable implications. Nothing prevented the teacher from planning the course in such a way that it would proceed from simple to more complicated matters; indeed this was what Franke and others recommended. Another reason is to show that the method or approach included the cultural aspect of language and also an element which could be described as empathy – for instance, as formulated by Franke (1884, p. 8): penetration into the way of thinking and the spirit of a foreign nation ('Eindringen in ein fremdes Denken, in einen fremden Volksgeist'). This is an idea which has been further developed in the present century (see section 7).

Despite Leonard Bloomfield's acknowledgement (1914, p. 293) of the success of the Reform Movement – 'It is only in the last twenty-five years and in the European countries that success in modern-language teaching has ever been attained' – the Direct Method never made much headway in the United States (Lado, 1964, p. 5; Hall, 1964, pp. 450–51). When finally during the Second World War linguists in America were called upon to provide intensive language instruction, the ideas that they incorporated in their courses 'stemmed almost in their entirety from the European reform movement of language teaching in the 1880s and 1890s' (Haugen, 1955, p. 243). Hence the puzzlement, and in some cases the despair, of teachers and linguists in Europe at what was confidently put forth after the war as new ideas under the umbrella of structural linguistics.

5 Structuralism and after

The chief idea as regards language teaching that may be said to have sprung directly from neo-Bloomfieldian structuralism is contrastive analysis of the source and target languages. This was advocated as a means of predicting the learner's difficulties, of identifying the points where there would be likely to be interference from the source language; and the remedy proposed was pattern drill to establish the right habits. In a less systematic way good teachers have probably always done something of this kind, but it is a valid criticism of courses designed on structuralist lines that their adherents seem to hold an exaggerated belief in the efficacy of contrastive analysis and drill as a cure for all ills. By no means all learners' errors are due to structural interference from the source language (Mackey, 1966). Secondly, there is reason to think that people do not in fact learn languages bit by bit (be they mother tongues or other tongues), but in large chunks. If each structural item had to be drilled and learnt separately, 'the child learner would be old before he could say a single appropriate thing and the adult learner would be dead' (Newmark, 1966, p. 78).

In other ways, too, the rather mechanistic approach of structuralist courses is open to criticism. These courses have not solved the problem of how to 'move from language manipulation to communication' (Prator, 1964). Divorced from a cultural context, from a situational meaning, pattern drills tend to become soulless and not very useful (Rivers, 1964). And although structuralists have often in their writings emphasized the importance of the cultural background – as when Fries (1955, p. 14) insisted that it must be 'an essential feature of every stage of language learning' – they have not, one feels, succeeded in bringing it into their courses in such a way as to capture and hold the students' interest. The empathy, or the attempt to instil it, is lacking. The most useful function of courses of this kind is probably as a supplement to other teaching; they are not self-sufficient, because learning a language is a great deal more than the acquisition of a mechanical skill.

The reaction against behaviourism in American linguistics initiated by Chomsky has also been reflected in ideas about language teaching. Some have thrown doubt on the usefulness of pattern drill, since 'the second-language learner could not possibly be drilled on an infinite variety of patterns' (Jakobovits, 1968, p. 106), and have advocated transformation exercises instead. As I. A. Richards (1967–8) has pointed out, there may be some confusion here between 'description' and 'thing described'. TG grammar purports to *describe* the language user's 'competence', that is, his ability to 'generate' and receive with understanding an infinite range of utterances; but it does not follow from this that TG grammar can also help the foreign learner to *acquire* that competence, or at least that it is any better for this purpose than any other kind of grammar. We still do not know enough about how languages are learnt. The value of recent research on first-language acquisition, which is open to doubt from this point of view, will be considered in another context (p. 45).

The interesting thing is that Chomsky's own position is quite different from that of his disciples. His utterances are unequivocal: 'I am, frankly, rather skeptical about the significance, for the teaching of languages, of such insights and understanding as have been attained in linguistics and psychology' (1966, p. 43). And further on: 'In general, the willingness to rely on "experts" is a frightening aspect of contemporary political and social life. . . . The field of language teaching is no exception. It is possible – even likely – that principles of psychology and linguistics, and research in these disciplines, may supply insights useful to the language teacher. But this must be demonstrated, and cannot be presumed' (p. 45). A few years later he said (1968, p. 690):

My own feeling is that from our knowledge of the organization of language and of the principles that determine language structure one cannot immediately construct a teaching programme. All we can suggest is that a teaching programme be designed in such a way as to give free play to those creative principles that humans bring to the process of language learning, and I presume to the learning of anything else. I think we should probably try to create a rich linguistic environment for the intuitive heuristics that the normal human automatically possesses.

Here we seem to be back at something like the Direct Method; and yet not completely, for a critical remark immediately afterwards about the modern emphasis on 'pronunciation ability' makes it clear that he had a different goal in mind from that of many language teachers.

6 Retrospect

Looking back over the history of language instruction in the last ninety years, one is filled with misgiving and a sense of malaise. We seem to have been marking time; perhaps we have even retrogressed. We are still plagued with a confusing array of methods; and experimental research on their relative merits is difficult because of the large number of variables involved, which are almost impossible to control. In most research schemes of this kind that have been undertaken in the United States, no very significant results have been obtained (see Carroll, 1966a, 1966b; Smith, 1970). A few years ago Politzer (1965, p. 12) confessed that 'From all the evidence it seems that relative success and failure of an individual in learning a language is not significantly influenced by the teaching method'. And success, it appears, is all too rare. But the malaise seems to be mainly or exclusively American. The situation in Europe is undoubtedly no worse and probably rather better than when Bloomfield acknowledged the success of the Direct Method.

On the reasons for the American lack of success one can but speculate. Carroll (1971a, p. 102) says that the field has been afflicted with many false dichotomies, such as that between 'habit' and 'rule-governed behaviour', and he says that 'the pressure of new fads and theories' tends to lead to a kind of professional panic among teachers. One does indeed get the impression that there has been much too uncritical a reliance on theory – or rather on conflicting theories, each with its band of faithful followers. Methods and theories have often been pitted against each other uncompromisingly, while the truth is probably somewhere in between. There seems to be an obsession with theory rather than practice. It is as if the proof of the pudding were no longer in the eating, nor in the recipe or the skill of the cook, but in the underlying nutritional or gustatory theory. It bothers Jakobovits (1970, p. 34) considerably that he cannot make the facts fit his theory: 'It would seem to be a betrayal of the intellectual spirit to accept that which works when it should not, yet it would be folly to reject that which works merely because on theoretical grounds it ought not'.

The uncertainty on the theoretical level may be a reflection rather than a cause of a generally unsatisfactory state of affairs in American language teaching. One difficulty on the North American continent is of course that the overwhelming majority of the population speak English, and those who speak other languages do not enjoy a very high social status. There is neither prestige nor utility to be gained from learning their languages, and consequently no great desire to do so. Unlike Europe, which is multilingual and multicultural, and where the need for a knowledge of other nations and their languages is obvious, especially in the smaller countries, the United States is almost entirely unilingual and unicultural, and there seems little incentive to bother about foreign languages.

7 Importance of attitude

In another part of the North American continent, in Montreal, the psychologist W. E. Lambert and his associates have carried out a series of researches on aspects of empathy, one of the qualities that are emphasized in the Direct Method (Lambert, 1963; Lambert *et al.*, 1968). The terms Lambert uses are motivation and attitude. There are two kinds of motivation, according to him, instrumental and integrative, the latter implying that the student wishes to gain inside knowledge of the target community as if in order to become a potential member. Experiments have shown that students with an integrative motivation, which of course means a favourable attitude to the people whose language they are trying to learn, are more successful than those who are merely instrumentally actuated. In particular they are better at acquiring a good accent. Lambert links this with O. H. Mowrer's theory of first-language learning, which asserts that the small child's learning is motivated by a basic desire to be like valued members of his environment. In the same way, Lambert argues, the learner of a second language must want to identify himself with members of the target community and be willing to take on very subtle aspects of their behaviour, including their style of speech.

It seems that this kind of integrative motivation is linked with a basic personality disposition. There is evidence that an 'authoritarian' attitude as it has been called – a tendency to self-sufficiency and prejudice against outsiders – is often reflected in poor second-language achievement (Lambert, 1963, p. 41; Gardner, 1966, pp. 27 and 41). A person who appears hopeless at languages is not necessarily lacking in the appropriate intellectual ability; it may be a personality trait that inhibits him; he may be resisting what seems to him an encroachment on his personality.

That the personality is involved in language learning should cause no surprise. All learning, all education of any kind, will affect a man's personality in some sort of way, his likes and dislikes, his system of values, his code of behaviour, his manners, etc. But intensive language learning will do so probably more than any other kind of training. First-language learning has a profound effect on the child; it is part of his socialization process whereby he becomes a member of his community and learns to accept its values and forms of behaviour, thus acquiring that part of his identity which marks him as belonging to that particular group. Second-language learning pursued in the way described above will have something of the same effect.

8 Language, culture and personality

There is in fact an indissoluble link between language and culture and hence personality. Language is in a sense part of a community's culture and at the same time the most important medium through which that culture is expressed. 'Culture' is of course used here in the anthropological sense to mean, not refinement of taste and intellect, but simply the way of life of a particular community, extending from its religious beliefs to its table manners. Culture in this sense is essential to the social well-being of the members of a community because it provides

a set of behaviour patterns that individuals brought up together recognize as the right and proper way of doing things. These behaviour patterns may be words, gestures, facial expressions; the knowledge of when to shake hands and when not to do so; all the various forms of greeting and the recognized responses to these forms; the method of giving and receiving orders and knowing which remarks are to be taken seriously and which are not. These and a whole host of others are essential elements in any culture, and they are as important to our composure as our religion or method of earning a living. They ensure that we feel at ease within our community (Gussman, 1960, pp. 243–4).

The cultural and social function of language has recently been restated by Hymes (1971, p. 278), who points out the inadequacy of a linguistic theory which consists solely of rules for linking referential meaning to sound, 'as if languages were never organized to lament, rejoice, beseech, admonish, aphorize, inveigh'. For our purpose the important thing about this social dimension is that any extended use of language will of necessity engage the user's personality.

It should not be forgotten that an individual's personality is only in part determined by hereditary factors; to a large extent it is a product of the culture, including the linguistic culture, of the community of people among whom he grows up or with whom he comes to associate himself fairly early in life (Sapir, 1962; Kluckhohn and Murray, 1948). In many ways a personality will only make sense in relation to the community that produced it; if judged by the standards of another community, a person's behaviour may be falsely assessed. For instance, what is accepted conduct in one community may be condemned as rude or aggressive in another; or what is normal in one community may be thought affected or sissy or fussy in another. Different communities attach different interpretations to such qualities as gentleness, modesty, aggressiveness, smartness, etc.

One more point should be made clear. Since the 'communities' that we are discussing here are most often, though not invariably, identical with nations as traditionally understood, it will be clear that anthropologists accept that there is such a thing as 'national character'. It is important to realize, however, that this term as used by anthropologists carries no implication of biological inheritance. Contemporary theories of culture and personality 'all agree that every culture has a typical personality which is characteristic and distinctive of that culture and which is produced or conditioned by some aspect of that culture' (Singer, 1961, p. 22). This view is very similar to older ideas about national character and the 'genius' of peoples; but there is the important difference that 'the units are now cultures rather than "races" or "peoples", and typical personalities are conceived as products of learning rather than of genetics' (Singer, 1961, p. 22).

It follows from what has been said that a person who has successfully learnt a second language by some form of 'integration' in Lambert's sense will have come to possess not only two languages but also two cultures; he will be bilingual and bicultural. I shall have more to say about these two concepts in a later chapter; here I must dwell a little on the related notion of linguistic relativity.

9 Linguistic relativity

This theory, which can be traced back at least to the eighteenth century, has been prominent in the minds of many language teachers since the Reform Movement of the 1880s. It asserts that a language influences the minds of those who use it and that consequently people using different languages classify their experiences differently and have different world pictures, different outlooks. Although many people – bilingual people of necessity – feel intuitively that there is an element of truth in the idea, proof is difficult to obtain. As Haugen said recently (in Alatis, 1970, p. 41), 'it feels different to talk one language than to talk another. You talk about different things and you talk about things from different points of view. The problem is how to capture this difference'. That there is a difference may, then, be taken for granted; it is in fact implied in what was said in section 8 about the close link between language and culture. Two relevant questions arise: In what part of language does this link reside, in the vocabulary or the grammatical structure? And is it not possible to learn a language without the accompanying culture?

It is self-evident that the vocabulary of a language is a good indicator of the culture of its speakers, their interests and beliefs and scale of values. A 'native-like' command of a language requires a 'native-like' feeling for the associations and connotative values of different words; otherwise the speaker is apt to sound off-key. The connotations of the English words *clever* and *smart*, which are not terms of unqualified praise and which have no very precise equivalents in related languages, are undoubtedly indicative of a culturally determined attitude. It is worth noting, too, that when one and the same language is used by culturally different communities, there will invariably be some differences in usage, chiefly in vocabulary (see, for example, Graham, 1956). Although it is probably true, as some have asserted, that any human language can be developed to express any human thought, it may mean stretching the language beyond what at any particular time is considered 'native-like' usage. Translators often have to resort to some degree of stretching.

Translators are sometimes up against other difficulties as well, 'as when the translation of Aristotle's philosophy into Arabic forced the choice, necessary in Arabic, between those copulas which indicated merely a connection and those which indicated a claim on existence, and led to differences in the interpretation of his thought in that language which were then passed on into medieval thought' (Hymes, in Alatis, 1970 p. 43). Here, of course, we are concerned with a point of structure, not of vocabulary; yet, as Hymes points out, systems of philosophy do, as a matter of demonstrable fact, pass from one language community to another. Any differences there may be in grammatical structure can never add up to a difference in world view.

The answer to the second question, about divorcing language and culture, is less simple. It is clear that communication across cultural boundaries can be difficult. A linguistic utterance removed from its proper cultural setting will at best sound off-key and at worst be devoid of meaning – or it may carry the wrong meaning – when seen from the point of view of the recipient's culture. Strictly, a language can have no meaning at all except in relation to some extralinguistic situation, some cultural context. All meaning is cultural. Linguists are fond of explaining that any utterance is a message which the receiver has to 'decode' according to the rules of the language. It is important to realize that he has to 'decode' it culturally as well. One might put it in a different way and say that any speaker has both a 'linguistic' and a 'cultural' accent (Soffietti, 1955), and either of them may be good or bad. Just as the linguistic accent may be hard to understand because it is foreign, so the cultural accent may be too 'thick' to be easily penetrable.

The theory of linguistic relativity has been hotly debated for years, often with emotional overtones. The idea that we might all in some way be imprisoned within our respective languages appeals to no one. But the important point is that we are not, even if we accept the theory. It is not a question of all or nothing. Systems of thought do cross language boundaries, because there are bilingual people who can open the prison-gates. The emotional reaction that some people show towards linguistic relativity may be linked with a belief in an absolute distinction between 'native' and 'foreign' in language, which would make an escape from the prison impossible – perhaps, too, with a pride in their own language and a refusal to believe that there could be distinctions which are not clearly and easily expressed in that language. Here, as over integrative motivation (p. 22), differences in personality and temperament may enter into the matter.

10 Implications for second-language learning

The implications of Lambert's theory for second-language learning are far-reaching. Not only must the learner want to become in imagination a member of the other community: if he persists in his learning he will end up, as has already been said, by being in a sense such a member, by belonging to two cultures. What starts as play-acting will end as a serious matter. If somebody tries over a period of years to think and act like a Frenchman, to seek his intellectual and emotional nourishment in the same way and from the same sources as a Frenchman, the end result will be that part of him will become French, French in spirit, and he could not suppress his Frenchness without damaging a vital part of his being. It will be part of his development as a person.

We are not here concerned with the question of whether full integration in the target community is possible (which will be discussed in chapter 3), nor whether it is desirable (which will be touched upon in chapter 5), but merely with ascertaining what it would involve. And here we have to admit that a clear-cut definition of the boundaries of culture for the purpose of language acquisition is impossible, just as it is impossible to give a precise definition of what is comprised under the term 'a full command' of a language (see section 20). Regular users of a language vary considerably in their general ability to handle the resources of the language, and in the same way they vary in their degree of familiarity with their own culture. There may also be idiosyncratic differences; some members of a community may reject certain aspects of its culture without ceasing to be members. In general, any knowledge, experience or belief which is shared by most members of a community may be said to be part of their culture and as such may be echoed or reflected in their use of the language.

Deutsch (1953) points out that in communicating with members of his own culture an individual will usually be able to predict the effect of his words by introspection. He will know how others are likely to react to them. Deutsch in fact suggests that 'predictability from introspection' might serve as a criterion for a nation. The second-language learner will need to develop some of the same ability to predict; he must expose himself to the community's ways and experiences and try to feel the effect of any message while standing in its shoes.

One aspect of culture which is particularly apt to be echoed in educated usage is literature. This may not be equally notice-able in all language communities, but it is a marked feature of English usage at a certain level. There is a core of literature known by most educated Englishmen and constantly drawn upon in one way or another, especially in writing but not uncommonly in speech as well. Sometimes this leads to direct verbal echoes, as when someone talks of 'protesting too much' or 'trailing clouds of glory'; at other times it produces more subtle and often unconscious reverberations of rhythms and clause-structures known from the classics. To use English satisfactorily at the intellectual level, to have a fully developed 'feeling' for the language, it is necessary to be familiar with this core of literature as well as with commonly known songs, nursery rhymes, traditional sayings, proverbs, etc. It is of course not an evaluation of these things as literature that is required, but first of all memorization and secondly an understanding of any emotional associations they may have. To avoid clichés it is necessary to know them well. The importance of this kind of study was recognized by Sir Denison Ross (1939).

A somewhat pessimistic note was struck by Sweet in an often-quoted passage in which he said that 'originality of mind does not make a good linguist. In fact, a talent for languages does not imply any higher intellectual development of any kind' (1899, p. 80). And he went on to say that he considered language acquisition to be to a great extent 'a mechanical process', in which originality of mind and a critical spirit were 'hindrances rather than helps'. What is higher and lower in matters of the mind is debatable, and what particular qualities of mind constitute a talent for languages has by no means been finally settled even now. A facility for imitating pronunciation may be part of it, but the ability to learn languages is certainly not an aptitude which is quite distinct from all other learning ability (Jakobovits, 1970, pp. 235–9; Wilkins, 1972, pp. 178–80). However, what Sweet did not seem to see, or accept, was that once a language has been learnt to a degree of proficiency that rivals the mother tongue – in fact he seemed to consider this to be impossible or unlikely to happen – its effective use requires the same degree of originality as all good speech and writing. A 'raid on the inarticulate' would be a good test of any learner's success, whether in a first or a second language.

Perhaps Sweet was influenced by a widespread attitude to mastery of a foreign language. It is generally conceded that somebody speaking or writing in his mother tongue is allowed to take liberties with the language, since after all 'it is his own language'. But somebody who had acquired the same language as a second language would be felt by many to be wrong to do the same; it would be an improper liberty for him to take, since 'it is not his own language'. Robert Graves said a few years ago of Vladimir Nabokov that 'his one error lies in arrogating a native-born's right . . . to do what he likes with the language' (1966, p. 49). There is of course no legal copyright in a language as such, but the proprietary feeling is widespread. Whether it is possible on biological or other scientifically valid grounds to substantiate a claim to ownership of a language by those who learnt it as infants is a question that will concern us in the next chapter. That the existence of this attitude to language may act as a barrier to successful second-language learning is obvious; the possible deterrent effect will be considered in chapter 4.

Most of what has been said up to now applies only to learners who are trying to acquire an all-purpose knowledge of a second language. But aims differ. Some people only want to be able to read the language, and others only to speak it. Others, again, may only want to learn the technical terms and phrases belonging to some specialized trade or profession, aerial navigation for instance. For the sake of simplicity, and since specialized courses give rise to few serious difficulties, this book will be mainly concerned with the process and problems of acquiring an all-purpose command of the target language in both speech and writing.

11 Some commonly made distinctions

A discussion of the meanings of some of the most commonly used labels in the field of language learning is necessary, and in fact long overdue in this book, in order to avoid misunderstandings. Some of the terms will be further discussed in the next chapter.

Many people use the term 'second' rather than 'foreign'

language. It is used in the title of this book and throughout the discussion, with the meaning simply of 'second-learnt'. It is opposed to 'first' language in the sense of 'first-learnt'. Neither term should be understood to carry any implication as to the user's proficiency in the language, because, as this book will argue, there is no direct connection between the order of learning and the relative importance of two languages later on in the user's life. A first language may be the mature person's primary or secondary medium, or it may be one that he has completely forgotten, having abandoned it at an early age. For obvious reasons, 'foreign' would be an unsuitable description for a second-learnt language which had become a primary medium. However, the distinction between primary and secondary media is by no means clear-cut; it will be discussed in chapter 4.

Some linguists and educators nowadays distinguish between a 'foreign' language, one which is studied for the insight it affords into the life of another nation, and a 'second' language, which is studied for more utilitarian reasons, because of its direct value to the speaker or writer as a citizen of his own country. This is by no means an absolute distinction (Pride, 1971, pp. 22–3); there are borderline cases and cases of transition from one group to the other. Up to a point, nevertheless, the distinction holds good, and it is often useful in discussing teaching aims and methods. The learner's attitude to a foreign language tends to be rather passive and receptive – though for true success it should not be (see section 7) – while to a second language it will – or should – be active and creative. A foreign language is used for the purpose of absorbing the culture of another nation; a second language is used as an alternative way of expressing the culture of one's own.

The distinction between 'second' and 'foreign' becomes clearer if it is seen in relation not to the individual speaker but to the whole community of speakers. Some countries accommodate more than one language community within their boundaries, and for the efficient functioning of the national life it is obviously important that a number of people, as many as possible, in each group should have a knowledge of the other language, or one or more of the other languages if there are several. Switzerland and Belgium and Finland are examples of countries where more than one language has official status. In other cases a minority language has no official status, and few speakers of the majority language, the official language, take the trouble to learn it, while those of the minority group will find it necessary to know the official language in addition to their own. The Breton and Basque languages in France are examples. In these cases 'second' is clearly a more appropriate term than 'foreign' for the additional language that has to be learnt. Many developing nations have problems of a similar kind (Fishman, Ferguson and Das Gupta, 1968).

Another situation that exists in some developing nations is one in which none of a number of indigenous languages can claim sufficiently wide support within the country as a whole to become recognized as official; instead an outside language, an 'exoglossic' one as it has been called (Kloss, 1968), is used as the official language, although no citizens speak it as their mother tongue. Nigeria and Ghana, in each of which countries English is the only official language, are examples. Exoglossic languages, then, form a subdivision under second languages, because to describe a country's official language as 'foreign' would appeal to no one but an agitator for recognition of one of the indigenous languages as official.

A somewhat different terminology has recently been proposed by Wilkins (1972), who would use the term 'second' language to describe the position, for example, of English in Nigeria and Ghana, where it is exoglossic, while for countries like Belgium, where each of the official languages is spoken by a substantial body of the population as their mother tongue, he would propose the term 'alternate' language. The difference, as he sees it, is that the learner of an alternate language has a much greater chance of prolonged contact with mother-tongue speakers and thus has a considerable advantage over the learner of a second language. He will often be much more at home in the language because he has heard it used in everyday life as well as for official purposes.

It will be less foreign to him than an exoglossic language.

The difficulty about this classification is that the situation that it describes is by no means uniform. Not many English-Canadians know French well, nor until recently was Flemish well-known among Walloons in Belgium. And, although French in relation to a Basque speaker would be 'alternate' in Wilkins's sense, the reverse would surely not be true. Moreover, how are we to classify the status of German in Switzerland (on which see also pp. 61 and 65), where the language that is used in everyday life by the German-Swiss is the Swiss variety (*Schwyzertütsch*), which is quite distinct from Standard German, the language that is used on all formal and official occasions? Is the latter then a 'second' language in Switzerland? What 'alternate' describes is a type of situation in which the motivation and opportunity to learn another language may range all the way from the optimal to the almost non-existent.

The phrase 'mother tongue' occurs as part of Wilkins's definition of an 'alternate' language. It has also been used once or twice in the preceding sections of this book. It is of course widely used in non-technical style to mean a person's 'best' language, which will usually be assumed to be also his 'first'. All three terms, 'best', 'first' and 'mother tongue', as well as the next one to be mentioned, 'native language', are often regarded as synonyms. 'Best' and 'first' require no further comment here, and 'native' will be mentioned below. 'Mother tongue' will be further discussed in the next chapter; meanwhile, our justification for using it has been the need to refer easily to a person's most intimate language, the one he feels most at home in and uses regularly in his private life, irrespective of how and when it was learnt. 'Primary language' might – and perhaps should – have been used instead.

Finally the term 'native'. This is often used as a synonym for a person's 'first' language, nearly always with the implication that it is his 'best' or 'primary' medium, which stands in a special relation to him, different from that of any other language; it is his 'own' language. It is a misleading term, because 'first' and 'best' are not invariably synonymous when applied to language, and the precise meaning of 'native' becomes correspondingly obscure. But the term is misleading for another reason as well: 'native' has etymologically something to do with birth, but no person is born with his language. There is indeed an innate element in language, the precise nature of which is still under discussion (see sections 15–17), but at least it does not extend to the practical command of a language. The meaning and use of 'native' will be further explored in section 21.

Of the various distinctions mentioned, the one that cuts deepest and is most significant, theoretically and practically, is undoubtedly that between a first and a later-learnt language. While all normal human beings learn one language, by no means everybody learns a second. Where a second language is learnt, irrespective of whether it is to be classified as 'foreign', 'second' or 'alternate', the fact that it is chronologically second means that special provision usually has to be made for it in the educational programme. Formal instruction needs to be given in both first and second-learnt languages if they are to be used well, especially for written purposes, but the form of the instruction will obviously differ somewhat. Moreover, the regular use of an additional, a second-learnt language, whatever its particular role and however learnt, gives rise to special problems, problems of bilingualism, which do not exist among unilingual people and which are consequently best considered together as constituting a special case. Throughout this book, therefore, 'second' is to be understood to mean simply chronologically second; the various subdivisions within that category will only be touched upon incidentally.

Three **Native and Foreign**

12 Popular and romantic notions about the mother tongue

There is a story – apocryphal no doubt – about a young
English couple who adopted a French baby and started to
brush up their French against the time when the baby would
begin to speak. Absurd though it is, the story probably contains a grain of truth, in that it reflects a feeling about language
with which few people can claim to be entirely unfamiliar.
Rational people of course dismiss the notion; there is plenty
of evidence to prove it wrong. But another notion which is
almost universally held is that there is something unique
about the 'mother tongue', the 'native' language. It is our
'own' language, imbibed in early childhood, effortlessly as it
seems, at least in retrospect. The fact that we can none of us
recall how we learnt our first language, while we can usually
remember something of the learning process of any later
language, may account for the almost instinctive division that
we are inclined to set up between native and foreign. Many
people distinguish between those who are 'native' speakers
of a language and those who have 'acquired' their knowledge
of it – as if we had never acquired our first language but had
somehow always had it.

Although instinctive reactions are not entirely to be spurned,
it is the duty of scholars and scientists to examine them
critically. If we followed our instincts blindly, we should still
believe that the earth is flat. Now the reason for the belief
that the earth is flat is easy enough to see; similarly it is not
hard to see how the 'native'–'foreign' distinction could have
arisen. Many older learners have difficulty in acquiring a good
accent, and so, however excellent their general command of

the language, they stand out as being different. Until the advent of phonetics in the late nineteenth century, few who learnt a second language in school acquired a 'native-like' accent. The relatively few who did, and the greater number who do so now, often passed or pass unnoticed – as many bilinguals prefer to do. And so the belief in an essential difference continues.

The instinctive belief in the mother tongue as something unique was undoubtedly reinforced, in medieval times and later, by romantic and sentimental ideas about motherhood, nurture and pristine innocence. If we believe that heaven lies about us in our infancy, it is but a short and natural step to thinking that anything that is acquired in infancy must also come from heaven. And so we may come to think of the mother tongue as a divine gift.

A somewhat different trend of thought and feeling underlies much romantic nationalist philosophy from the late eighteenth century onwards (Borst, 1957–63, pp. 1521 ff.). By the miracle of Pentecost, God sanctioned the use of the mother tongue for religious instruction. He it was who created the nations and set the bounds of their habitation, and He it was who gave to each nation its separate tongue. God speaks to the people of each land through the translation of the Bible into the language that they can understand, which thus becomes His language as well as theirs. In many countries, furthermore, the translation of the Bible has helped to standardize the language and lay the foundations of a national literature, through which the nation now expresses its peculiar spirit and character; and so in a semi-mystical way nation, fatherland, language, literature and religion come to form an indissoluble unity.

Although, perhaps, few people nowadays would agree with this way of thinking in its entirety, to many there is something sacred about the mother tongue because it is part of the national heritage, and it is a sacred duty, they feel, to love and cherish that heritage. Whether we should understand *sacred* in this context to mean merely 'of gravest importance', or whether the nation as such is to be thought of as invested with divine authority, the word clearly suggests something that transcends the individual.

Others who also regard the matter as of gravest importance would place the emphasis differently, as in the following quotation from a Colonial Office paper (1927, pp. 4–5) on the place of the vernacular in African education:[1]

The mother tongue is the true vehicle of mother wit. Another medium of speech may bring with it, as English brings with it, a current of new ideas. But the mother tongue is one with the air in which a man is born. It is through the vernacular (refined, though not weakened, by scholarship and taste) that the new conceptions of the mind should press their way to birth in speech. This is almost universally true, except in cases so rare (like that of Joseph Conrad) as to emphasize the general rule. A man's native speech is almost like his shadow, inseparable from his personality. In our way of speech we must each, as the old saying runs, drink water out of our own cistern. For each one of us is a member of a community. We share its energy and its instincts; its memories, however dim, of old and far-off things. And it is through our vernacular, through our folk-speech, whether actually uttered or harboured in our unspoken thoughts, that most of us attain to the characteristic expression of our nature and of what our nature allows us to be or to discern. Through its mother tongue the infant first learns to name the things it sees or feels or tastes or hears, as well as the ties of kindred and the colours of good and evil. It is the mother tongue which gives to the adult mind the relief and illumination of utterance, as it clutches after the aid of words when new ideas or judgements spring from the wordless recesses of thought or feeling under the stimulus of physical experience or of emotion. Hence in all education the primary place should be given to training in the exact and free use of the mother tongue.

In this passage there is no suggestion of duty towards anybody or anything outside the individual himself, unless it be towards some sort of universal truth. And yet the tone is exalted, and the style almost quivers with emotion. Although the subject-matter falls within the realm of things that are open to scientific inquiry, the treatment could not be described as sober, let alone scientific. An amusing instance of this is

[1] The ultimate source of the quotation is the report of the Calcutta University Commission (1919).

the phrase 'sees or feels or tastes or hears'; scientific accuracy requires the addition of 'or smells', or complete rewriting. The many metaphors and veiled and vague terms make it a difficult passage to discuss. Undoubtedly it contains an element of truth, but also something which a rational inquiry could not uphold. The anonymous writer might retort, in reply to these remarks, that he was not attempting to write scientifically; he was using an emotional style because that seemed to him an appropriate way of dealing with this matter which concerns the innermost core of a person's being. But this imaginary reply would only corroborate our earlier contention (section 1) that there are areas in which our thinking about language is mystical rather than scientific. And it might, and should, be pointed out that the aim of the paper of which the passage forms part was to arrive at an objectively valid basis for policy making.

By and large, it seems, the purport of the passage is to stress the view expressed in section 8 of the present book about the close link between language, culture and personality. So far so good, but the reference to Joseph Conrad shows that the writer identifies mother tongue with 'first-learnt language', and he sees in this identification an inevitability which appears to be part of man's nature or the universal scheme of things rather than a product of environmental factors. It is to be regretted that he does not tell us how he would fit Conrad into his picture, because in scientific work even apparent exceptions have to be accounted for. This omission is all the more regrettable since cases of this kind, in which a second-learnt language has come to be used as a person's main or only medium of expression, are far more common than the anonymous writer seems to imagine. There are innumerable such cases among immigrants and descendants of immigrants in America, and there are many in Britain, especially among people with a Welsh or Gaelic background. Not all of these become writers, but a fair proportion do (Haugen, 1956, p. 71). Some become distinguished in other areas of national life involving great skill in the use of language; examples are Lloyd George, the politician, and Emlyn Williams, the actor.

As Leonard Forster (1970) demonstrates, until the Romantics invested each nation's language with a soul, people had a much less developed sense of what linguists nowadays call 'language loyalty'. In earlier centuries it was by no means uncommon for the same individual to use more than one language for literary purposes.

13 'Mother tongue' and related terms

A belief that a person's language is in some way given him at birth is of considerable antiquity. We find it reflected in the terms that are used. Within our western tradition we find phrases in classical Latin like *'sermo in quo nati sumus'* (lit. 'the language in which we are born': Krebs and Schmalz, 1905–7, s.v. *maternus*). Bede (AD 731) echoes this when he talks of scholars who know the Latin and Greek languages as well as they know their own in which they were born, *'propriam in qua nati sunt'* (book 4, chapter 2), or the language of their birth, *'nativitatis suae loquelam'* (book 5, chapter 23). We are told by Frutolf (*Chronicon Universale*, AD 1099) that Godfrey of Bouillon spoke both French and German with native-like (or innate?) skill: *'per innatam sibi utriusque linguae peritiam'*. Phrases like *natale ydioma* (Sunesen c. 1210, quoted by Kristensen, 1926, p. 69) and *nativa lingua* are met with in medieval writings; the latter is found in Higden's *Polychronicon* (1352) in a well-known passage about the languages of Britain. In John of Trevisa's translation of that passage (1385: Mossé, 1952, pp. 287–8) the phrase has become 'birth-tongue', a term which does not appear to have been used by any other writer. Since the beginning of the sixteenth century the term 'native language' has been in common use in English (see Oxford English Dictionary).

Terms linking language with birth are found in most and possibly all European languages, east and west, and more or less synonymous phrases are found in many parts of the world outside Europe. That the attitude which these terms represent may not be entirely universal has been suggested by Hill (1970), as was mentioned earlier (section 4).

On the other hand, the term mother tongue appears to have

arisen in western Europe in historical times. It is found nowadays in the Romance and Germanic areas, in the Slavonic world outside Russian and White Russian, and in languages like Hungarian, Finnish and Lappish, which almost certainly borrowed it from their neighbours.

Attempts have been made by Kristensen (1926) and Weisgerber (1938) to prove that 'mother tongue' is a Germanic formation, but the most convincing theory appears to be that represented by Spitzer (1948), who argues that the term arose on Romance soil early in the twelfth century in the form of medieval Latin *lingua materna*. The nearest equivalent in classical Latin was *sermo patrius*, 'ancestral language'. The change from *sermo* to *lingua* was due to the semantic development of the former word in medieval Latin, but the change in adjective appears to have had a deeper significance. *Lingua materna* came into use to denote the language of infancy and early childhood, the home language as distinct from the scholar's Latin, *lingua litterata*. Dante in *De vulgari eloquentia* used the phrase *materna locutio* (book 1, chapter 6), and described the latter language as nobler than Latin, 'because it is natural to us, while the other is rather of an artificial kind' ('*quia naturalis est nobis, cum illa potius artificialis existat*') (book 1, chapter 1).

Characterization of the vernacular as the natural language, *lingua naturalis*, is found sporadically throughout the medieval period and later. Bede, for instance, mentions a certain scholar who knew Latin as well as he did the English language, 'quae sibi naturalis est' (book 5, chapter 20), and Rabelais's Panurge calls French his '*langue naturelle et maternelle*' (1532, chapter 9). From the end of the thirteenth century the more emotionally coloured phrase *lingua materna*, until then fairly rare, became increasingly common (Borst, 1957–63, p. 826), and in the fourteenth century we find it translated into a number of national languages, Romance and Germanic, as, for instance, *parlar materno* (Dante) and *modyr tonge* (Wyclif).

The development of the term *lingua materna* appears, then, to be indicative of the widening gulf in the Romance world between vernacular speech and the literary language. But the strong emotional connotations that the phrase possesses seem to derive primarily from other sources: from the awakening of national consciousness in medieval times, from a prevailing feeling in medieval Christendom about the position of woman and of the mother in particular, and from the symbolic associations of motherhood, nurture and milk. Instruction whether in religious or secular matters in the Middle Ages was often described metaphorically in terms of motherly care, as in *Alma Mater*. And of course we still talk of 'mother wit' and of imbibing things 'with the mother's milk'.

After this brief excursion into word history, we shall resume our quest for early ideas on heredity in language.

14 Early scientific ideas on linguistic heredity

There was a time when it was thought that babies were born with an innate knowledge of a particular language, though not necessarily that of their parents. In the seventh century BC, according to Herodotus (book 2, chapter 2), the Pharaoh Psammetichus conducted an experiment to find out which was the most ancient nation. Two new-born babies were isolated; they were looked after well, but nobody was allowed to utter a word in their presence. The plan was to note what language they would begin to speak spontaneously. After two years they were heard to utter the word *bekos* (βεκος), which was identified as the Phrygian word for bread. And so, reluctantly perhaps, the Egyptian experimenters concluded that the Phrygian nation was of greater antiquity than any other.

The unproved assumption on which this conclusion rests is that there is a difference between a man's true language and that which he learns in infancy: in other words, between nature and nurture, between heredity and environment. This idea may have been linked with some belief in pre-existence and reincarnation. A secondary premiss of an empirical kind was the observation that the environment always wins. Consequently the aim of the experiment was to exclude this factor.

As far as it went, the experiment may be said to have been successful. A modern linguist would of course feel that a great deal more than one word would be needed to enable us to identify a language. This and perhaps a lingering doubt about the underlying assumption may account for two repetitions of the experiment that have been recorded. One of these was conducted by the Emperor Frederick II of Hohenstaufen (reigned 1212–50), who approached the experiment with a somewhat more open mind: 'He wanted to find out whether [the children] would speak the Hebrew language, which was the oldest, or perhaps Greek or Latin or Arabic, or simply the language of their parents of whom they had been born' (Salimbene, *Cronica*, AD 1250, p. 510, trans. by Paul Christophersen). But he laboured in vain, says Salimbene, who described the whole idea as '*superstitio*'; the children all died. James IV of Scotland repeated the experiment, probably in the year 1493, by placing two young children on the island of Inchkeith in the charge of a dumb woman. As for the result, an unconfirmed report has it that the children 'spak goode hebrew'; but, as the modern editor says, at that date few people in Scotland knew Hebrew, let alone what was good Hebrew (Pitscottie, c. 1576, vol. 1, p. 237 and vol. 2, p. 374).

The idea that Hebrew was mankind's original language was widespread in medieval times. Dante, for example, expressed it in *De vulgari eloquentia* (book 1, chapters 6–7), in which he described Hebrew as a *sanctum idioma* given to Adam with the creation of his soul. This belief survived for centuries. When a boy of about twelve, the so-called 'Wild Boy of Aveyron', was discovered in 1797 running about completely naked in the forests of the Massif Central, unable to speak, and it became clear that he must have lived most of his life outside human society, there were some who expected to hear from his mouth mankind's original language: 'they conjectured that it was most likely to be Hebrew' (Brown, 1958, p. 3). The boy never in fact learnt to speak, although he was given special tuition and lived in Paris at government expense till he died in 1828 (Malson, 1972).

It is regrettable that, in the days when no ethical considerations stood in the way of man's thirst for knowledge, he should have conducted his researches with so little success.

We would indeed give a great deal nowadays to possess the answer that those early experiments attempted to provide. On the basis of such evidence as there is, we imagine that we have an answer, but an element of uncertainty attaches to it (see section 17).

15 Darlington

There is no evidence that a person is born with a latent mastery of one particular language. In fact everything points to the conclusion that this is not so; any knowledge a person may have of a particular language comes from his surroundings. Nevertheless, there is a theory that a person may have an innate preference for specific linguistic features, characteristic of one language rather than another. This theory, the so-called 'substratum theory', has been used to explain linguistic changes, especially sound changes. Thus it is frequently and perhaps universally the case that, where a language shift occurs, where a whole population changes over from one language to another, as from Irish to English in Ireland, certain features of the earlier language, the substratum, are carried over into the new. This transference could be accounted for simply as due to imperfect learning and not inability to learn, which would make it easier to explain why there will nearly always be some individuals who achieve perfection. But a particular form of the theory assumes that such changes could skip one or more generations before they appear – in other words, that there is an element of biological inheritance involved.

The theory originated among linguists trying to account for certain historical changes. The evidence from historical linguistics was later reviewed by Jespersen (1922, pp. 191–201), who considered it not very strong, and who in any case rejected the idea of heredity on the grounds that 'words and sounds are nothing but habits acquired by imitation'. But the theory was revived twenty-five years later by a geneticist, C. D. Darlington (1947) who, pointed out an apparent coincidence between blood-group distribution in Europe and the occurrence of dental fricatives. This discovery would seem to have implications which go far beyond the use of that particular sound. The case for heredity along these lines has since been examined by Brosnahan (1961), in whose formulation it amounts to the assumption of a hereditary predisposition in each mating group for some particular complement of linguistic features, especially sounds. But Brosnahan emphasizes (p. 30) that the biological inheritance will not prevent any one individual from acquiring a perfect command of a language other than that of his parents. In this form the theory can hardly have any relevance to the present discussion.

16 Human versus animal communication

In recent years interest in the biological element in language has shifted its focus, which is now less on the features that distinguish one language from another than on universal linguistic features, those that all human languages have in common and which distinguish them from animal types of communication. The hereditary factor in linguistic diversification, if there is one, is elusive and of doubtful importance, for differences between languages appear to be primarily traditional. On the other hand, differences such as those between human and animal systems of communication are clearly species-specific; they are bound up with biological differences, although early experience could also play some part – experience, that is, specific to the species. Despite some recent remarkable but limited success in teaching chimpanzees human language (Gardner and Gardner, 1971; Premack, 1971), no animal has yet mastered a human form of communication. And despite what we have discovered about communication among bees, we cannot confidently say that we have fully cracked the code of any animal form of communication.

An important difference between human and animal communication is the greater role of biological inheritance in the latter. Insect communication appears to be almost entirely instinctive; dialects occur, but they seem to be genetically determined (Carthy, 1966). In some forms of birdsong too, for example that of the blackbird, there is apparently no tradition, no element of learning (Haldane, 1956). But certain other birds, especially the skylark and the chaffinch, must learn their song. Reared in isolation, the skylark is said to produce an unrecognizable song, and the chaffinch a crude and imperfect one – but even in its imperfection characteristic of the species and hence genetically determined. Owing to the element of learning there are dialects among the chaffinches. The Cambridge chaffinch sings a different song from that of the Somerset chaffinch, and the chaffinches in the Azores sing a dialect differing far more from any of the British dialects than the latter differ among themselves (Haldane, 1956; McNeill, 1970; Bateson, 1972). Whether the gap between human and animal communication has always been as wide as it is now is a matter for conjecture; Haldane suggests that the language of man or his ancestors may once have had a far larger element of the instinctive in it.

17 Chomsky and Lenneberg

Chomsky and his associates have given a great deal of attention to the innate element in language, that part of language which is species-specific as distinct from that which is learnt. They assume that a human being is endowed by nature with a capacity for learning a system of communication of the particular type which we find in human languages. This capacity, sometimes referred to as the Language Acquisition Device,[2] includes the power to abstract and 'internalize' unconsciously the structural rules underlying raw language material to which the child is exposed.

It is assumed that without such exposure no learning will take place. The evidence for this consists partly of so-called 'wolf children', children isolated from human society and left to the care of animals. A number of such cases have been

2. Thus Chomsky (1965). But Chomsky also uses various other phrases to describe the innate element, notably 'tacit knowledge of linguistic universals' (1965, p. 27). It would sidetrack the present discussion to pursue the philosophical implications of the latter phrase. For our purpose the above term, or 'system of mechanisms' (1967, p. 84) or 'instinctive capacity' (1967, p. 86), is more appropriate.

recorded in the course of human history (Malson, 1972), the best-known being the 'Wild Boy of Aveyron' (see section 14). From a consideration of all the evidence it seems pretty clear that, if for some reason a new-born baby is removed from human society, it will not acquire speech. The innate capacity for language learning will be given no material to work on. Moreover, there is further evidence, partly from the language development of deaf children, to suggest that a so-called 'critical period' exists, extending up to the age of puberty, during which time the individual is in a state of readiness for first-language learning (Lenneberg, 1967). It is during this period that the specific brain mechanisms that acquire and control language are developed, a process which is part of the general maturation of the brain. If a child is not exposed to a human language during this period, the innate capacity will atrophy and the ability to learn any language will be lost for ever.

A great deal of research has been done in recent years on the early stages of normal first-language acquisition up to the age of about three. This has revealed a striking regularity in the various stages through which the learning process passes, cooing and babbling, one-word utterances, two-word utterances, and finally complete sentences. Not only the sequence but the timing of the onset of the various stages is remarkably uniform, thus supporting the idea that the process is genetically determined and not to be explained merely as imitation of adult speech. In fact, children who for one reason or another (disease, neglect, etc.) have missed out one or more of these stages will begin, in response to treatment, to talk in accordance with their age level (Lenneberg, 1967, pp. 140–41). Still it is important for our present purpose to bear in mind that what we are witnessing in studying these early stages of language development is merely the 'maturation of instinctive capacity before it reaches the appropriate time' (Chomsky, 1967, p. 86), the appropriate time being when normal competence has been achieved. Since second-language learning does not usually begin until the instinctive capacity has reached some degree of maturity, our knowledge of the early stages of first-language learning provides no clue to any later learning process. Almost the only certain statement we can make about the latter is that it does not proceed through the various early stages of first-language learning.

It used to be thought by many linguists that by the age of four or five the normal child would have learned all the basic rules of his language. It has since become clear that some aspects of grammar are not acquired until much later, if they are acquired at all. Carroll (1971b, pp. 148–9) puts it as follows:

Although a substantial degree of basic competence in the rules of the native language is attained by the normal child at school-entry age, development is by no means complete at that time. Certain advanced stages of phonology are not normally mastered until about eight years of age, and it is probably the case that complete competence in the grammatical rules of the language is not approximated until the period of adolescence, and even this statement must be qualified to apply only to the competence assumed as a basis for spoken performance, since a substantial number of adolescents do not seem able to manifest adequate grammatical competence in written performance. In the lexical and semantic aspects of linguistic competence, development is highly incomplete at school entry.

But although in a sense learning continues throughout a person's life, there may be some basis for regarding the age of four or five as something of a milestone in language acquisition, marking the completion of a certain stage of development. By this time the child is not only able to put together correct sentences of a fairly wide range of patterns in his first language; he is also able in a remarkably short time to learn to do the same in another language if he is exposed to it. In fact, if the environment changes completely, after a few months the child will have forgotten the first language, and he will very soon learn to handle the second in a manner which is indistinguishable from that of a first-language learner.

Another milestone, as suggested by Lenneberg and others, may be found at the end of the postulated critical period, at the age of puberty. Beyond this point, Lenneberg holds (1967, p. 176), the power of automatic acquisition from mere exposure to a language seems to disappear, although he admits that a person of forty *can* learn to communicate in a foreign language. Braine (1971, pp. 70–72) contends that the evidence for this view – the popular view – is very weak; it consists almost entirely of the observation that those who learn a second language after puberty often speak it with a foreign accent. This may indicate, he says, the loss of some special facility at the phonological level, but there is no indication that it extends to other areas of language. Mrs Ervin-Tripp (in Kelly, 1969, p. 26) points to a psychological difference when she says that 'for children under eleven language is sound, for adults, sense'; children are more interested in the surface and the immediate situation. Thus it has frequently been observed that some adults spend long periods in a foreign country without picking up the language; this is probably, Braine thinks, because they feel less highly motivated to learn than a child who is sent to school in a foreign country. And the fact that grown-ups, when they do decide to learn, mostly use different methods is no proof, he says. 'The adult can rarely afford the time the child spends, and the educated adult has resources available in the form of written materials and formal instruction in the language, which increase the efficiency of learning. However, illiterate adults learn new languages when they have to; they presumably face essentially the same task that children do, that of discovering the structure of the language on the basis of spoken text materials. There is no evidence that they solve this task in a substantially different way than do children.' And Braine sums up: 'If there is a decline in language-learning ability with age, it looks as if it is probably a slow decline associated with middle and old age, not with adolescence.' It should be added that any such decline with age may be due in part to difficulties of personality adjustment (see section 19).

The fact remains, however, that pronunciation difficulties seem to increase after puberty. It is still possible after that age to learn a good, and even a perfect, pronunciation of a foreign language, but it usually requires special instruction – which it is now possible to give with the help of phonetics. As has been suggested earlier, the popular idea that there is an essential difference between 'native' and 'foreign' speakers may have sprung from the obvious difficulties that many adults have with foreign speech sounds. Two points should be made here. In the first place, many speakers, if they are sufficiently highly motivated, are able long after puberty to modify an original dialect or regional accent in their first language in the direction of the national standard, if there is one; and from a linguistic point of view there is no essential difference between a foreign and a dialect accent. Secondly, as has already been observed, a person's general learning of his first language continues throughout life, and there is no evidence that the learning of a second language is any different in this respect.

18 Penfield

It is in part the child's facility in learning pronunciation that underlies an idea about language teaching which was put forward some years ago by Wilder Penfield, a brain surgeon (Penfield and Roberts, 1959; Penfield, 1963). Like many other workers in this field, Penfield had noticed that a child's brain appears to be more plastic than a grown-up's in the sense that, if injury or disease destroys the speech areas of a child, control of the speech mechanism can be successfully transferred to the other hemisphere of the brain. In the case of an adult person an entirely successful transfer is much less certain. A further observation to which Penfield attaches importance is that electrical stimulation during a brain operation will sometimes prompt an adult patient to have vivid impressions of scenes which he says belong to his past life (Penfield, 1958). This has led Penfield to infer that little or nothing that has once been the focus of attention is ever again erased from the brain. From these two observations Penfield concludes that if children are taught foreign languages early and thus acquire a good accent, the 'speech units' will be 'hidden away in the brain', waiting to be employed when language instruction is resumed later in the school career. On the other hand, says Penfield (Penfield and Roberts, 1959, p. 255), 'when languages are taken up for the first time in the second decade of life, it is difficult, though not impossible, to achieve a good result.'

Various objections can be raised against Penfield's view. In the first place, we do not know enough about the long-term effects of early second-language learning. For instance, we need an answer to the question, 'How much of early-acquired language competence is forgotten with disuse, and how easily can it be reacquired?' (Carroll, 1961, p. 48). Penfield instances his own son, who found that a period of three months spent in a Spanish school when he was five helped him at the age of thirty in relearning Spanish (1963, pp. 134–5). But others have been less successful in recalling past experience. After all, Penfield's patients needed prodding with an electric wire during an operation before their early memories returned. And the return was entirely random; no method has been devised, not even one involving an operation, which can ensure the willed recall from the subconscious mind of a particular past experience or piece of knowledge. It should be noted, too, that Penfield's patients were suffering from epilepsy, and we cannot be sure that a healthy brain would react in a similar manner (Wooldridge, 1963, p. 168); we are not even sure that the alleged early memories were true memories. Secondly, we need to remember that, unless brain damage occurs, the lack of plasticity does not markedly affect the functioning of the speech centres of an older person. Penfield claims that to start learning a new language after puberty is difficult because it is 'unphysiological', whatever that may mean (Penfield and Roberts, 1959, p. 255; cf. Newmark and Reibel, 1968, p. 154). But, as pointed out before, pronunciation difficulties after the age of puberty can be successfully overcome by expert training, and as regards other aspects of usage the advantage lies probably with the older child or adolescent. It must not be forgotten that successful learning even of the first language continues long after early childhood and after puberty, and it is not until a person is eighteen or twenty that he can be said to have a reasonably full command. Increasing difficulty with age in learning another language may be due primarily to other factors, such as lack of time and patience and, even more, consolidation of the personality (see section 19).

Finally, it is important to realize that Penfield links his plea for early language instruction with a strong recommendation that it should be carried out by the Direct Method and not 'with word lists, and grammar and syntax' (1963, p. 130), which he considers to be an inefficient way. He says, moreover, that the Direct Method can succeed even in adult teaching, and he mentions Joseph Conrad as an example of a person who learnt English in that way at a relatively advanced age. It appears, then, that the specifically neurological part of Penfield's case is weak if it is at all relevant.

19 Recapitulation

There seems no clear scientific evidence for regarding a second-learnt language as being in an essentially different relationship to the learner by the mere fact of being second in order of learning. 'Native' and 'foreign', if defined simply in terms of chronology, cannot be upheld as a clear-cut distinction. It is probably true that small children find language learning easier than adolescents and adults, but it would be hard and perhaps impossible to fix a final age limit beyond which it is no longer possible to acquire a good knowledge of another language. The term 'good' is used here deliberately in order not to prejudge the question of 'perfection', which will be considered in the next section.

The increasing difficulty with age that some people experience could conceivably, though not very probably, be linked with the hardening of the speech centres in the brain that Penfield and others have observed, but certainly there are other and more important factors involved (Haugen, 1956, p. 73). The small child is unformed as a person and is keen to model his behaviour on that of his elders in order to become a member of their social group; but gradually a consolidation of the personality sets in which may inhibit the kind of submission to a new model that second-language learning requires. Moreover, it may be difficult for the older person to see the necessity for the effort required, since he is already a member of a social group. Experience in Canada with immigrant children aged twelve to eighteen shows that the basic problem in teaching them English is to provide them with the need and the opportunity to identify themselves with the new culture and its value system. Once that has been done, the language is learnt easily and quickly (Gladstone, 1967). Lambert's work with university students in Montreal (see section 7) confirms the importance of a desire for integration.

20 Relative proficiency

Can one learn to use a foreign language with the same ease and fluency as one's first language? Put like that, the question is hard to answer without certain reservations. In the first place, we need to be clear as to whether 'foreign' excludes 'second' and 'alternate' languages, in the more technical sense of these terms mentioned in section 11. Languages in the last two groups, and particularly 'alternate' languages, are often handled with a high degree of mastery. Secondly, we need to know what is meant by 'first'. In some cases a first-learnt language will only belong to a brief phase in a child's development and has to be discounted for the purpose of this argument. For instance, parents stationed abroad sometimes find that their small children pick up the local language from a nanny or from playmates before they learn to speak their parents' language. If the family returns to its own country after a year or two, this first-learnt language will usually, in a remarkably short time, vanish without trace from the children's memory. If, on the other hand, the family remains in its foreign station, the two languages will probably become competitors and their precise relationship will depend on a number of factors to be discussed in chapter 4.

Usually, however, what is in the mind of someone asking that question is whether a language started as an ordinary school subject and learnt mostly or entirely in that way can ever be brought to a pitch of proficiency equivalent to what is achieved in the so-called mother tongue. Here, too, a number of reservations need to be made. A great deal, obviously, will depend on the teacher and on the availability of audiovisual and other aids. Secondly, and more importantly, a strong motivation, as mentioned in section 19, needs to be present. Thirdly, although a good teaching programme, combined with an imaginary approach, will in part dispense with the necessity for a stay in surroundings where the target language is habitually used, obviously such a stay is a great help in consolidating what has been learnt (Christophersen, 1957). Finally, it needs to be realized that learning a language, whether first or second, is a long-term project. It is eternally true, as Sweet said (see p. 12), that there is no royal road to mastery of a language. A well-planned second-language course will naturally condense the material a good deal to enable the pupil to absorb it in a reasonably short time; but even so it will probably be quite a few years before the learner reaches a stage when he can no longer be easily distinguished from a so-called native speaker.

Since knowledge of a language and of the way of life of its speakers go hand in hand, it may be thought that a man who has spent all his life in one country will have a degree of familiarity with that country which no amount of intensive study by an outsider can make up for. But nobody knows all aspects and areas of his nation's life; a great deal of what a resident knows, or thinks he knows, is acquired at second-hand through the news media, friends, etc. Perhaps he knows only a small area really well and the rest by some kind of extrapolation. An outside learner can do something similar after a few years' residence. Even some of the experience of childhood can be recreated. It is sometimes said (e.g. by Sweet, 1899, p. 76) that an older child or a grown-up starting to learn a second language will experience some difficulty because his maturity is far in excess of the sort of foreign-language material that he is able to handle in the initial stage. A learner with a genuine capacity for empathy has usually no such difficulty; he will in imagination 'start as a child and grow up again' (Fries, 1955, p. 19), and childish language, nursery rhymes, etc., are part of his experience of the other nation, part of the new personality or extension to his personality that he is building up.

In deciding whether perfection is possible in a second language, it has to be borne in mind that measuring language competence – in the general rather than the Chomskyan sense of the word – is no simple matter (see section 23). With what is it to be compared? A bilingual person's two languages will seldom be completely in balance. Most often one will be dominant in relation to the other, and it may well be the second-learnt language that is the stronger, at least within certain fields of interest or activity – for instance, in writing as opposed to speech. Or are we to compare the competence in each language with that of a unilingual speaker of that language? But no two people have exactly the same command of their mother tongue; one person will be found to be weaker in one area and one in another, depending largely on their experience and interests, and on their degree of education. Numerous tests have been carried out on aspects of bilingual proficiency, including relative performance of bilinguals and unilinguals (for references see section 23). Owing to the uncertainty about definitions and the difficulty of controlling the many variables involved, no simple answer has been found; nor could one have been expected. It has been observed that a person's reaction time to linguistic messages is sometimes shorter in a second than in a first language (Lambert, 1956), and this has been held to show greater 'automaticity' and thus to be a sign of a shift of dominance from the first to the second language. Other tests, involving various forms of verbal behaviour, have confirmed this view (Lambert *et al.*, 1959). There is also evidence that in some cases a second language has come to hold stronger emotional associations.

From what has been said it will be clear that 'perfection' in a language, first or second, is not something clear-cut and absolute. Beyond a certain stage of proficiency it may be futile or meaningless to ask whether a learner has a 'perfect' command. The best definition of 'perfect' is probably 'indistinguishable from a native speaker', but that raises the question of how to define 'native' (see section 21) and how to determine the range of proficiency that may exist among native speakers. Moreover, in practice we find it hard at the advanced stage to assess a person's linguistic and cultural accents separately (see p. 26). As Brosnahan says (1960, pp. 92–3), our judgement of whether somebody is English or not is influenced very considerably by attendant circumstances: a person who speaks what seems normal English and whose physical appearance, dress and deportment, views and beliefs, etc., fall within the range of what from previous experience we expect from native-born-and-bred Englishmen, will tend to be classed as English by other Englishmen, and a single peculiarity in his use of the language is likely to be accepted as an addition to our general knowledge of present-day usage rather than as a sign that he is not English. It takes more than one deviation to arouse our suspicion, and cultural criteria are as important as linguistic ones in arousing or allaying such a feeling.

In trying to pick out a foreigner whose language seems perfect, many people resort by preference to cultural criteria. Sometimes, despite an apparently perfect linguistic accent, the cultural one may show foreign influence. The speaker may have overlooked some detail in the cultural scene; or, alternatively, he may be deliberately withholding his personality and not fully accepting the way of life of the target community in order to avoid a conflict with his first-acquired culture (see p. 79); or he may have idiosyncratic reasons for deviating slightly from the usual pattern of behaviour. Reaction to this kind of behaviour varies considerably; but it resembles in some ways a common reaction to linguistic deviationism (p. 29): inadvertent oversight is easier to accept than deliberate eccentricity. Views about those 'not to the manner born' are probably due less to a belief in heredity than to an idea that it is early training that counts and that earns one the right to membership, and that after a certain age no one can – or should – reach perfection, whether in language or in way of life.

21 Appropriateness of terminology

Linguists, like laymen, customarily distinguish between the language a person learns first, his mother tongue or native language, and any language or languages he may learn later in life (e.g. Hughes, 1962, pp. 19–21). The precise definition of 'native' varies and is not always clear. Some would stress the importance of priority of learning, while others merely say that a language to be called 'native' must have been learnt in childhood without formal instruction; in the latter case, consequently, one may talk of 'childhood acquisition of two or more native languages' (Diebold, 1961, p. 99).

Other linguists, to avoid the emotional connotations of 'mother tongue' etc., prefer the terms 'L1' and 'L2'. As originally introduced by Catford (1959, p. 165), the term 'L1' meant primary language – that is, 'the language of its speaker's intimate daily life' – and was not necessarily identical with the first-learnt language. But others have associated the term with 'first'. Others, again, merely emphasize that the learning must have taken place in early childhood. Thus although Halliday, McIntosh and Strevens (1964, p. 78) admit the difficulty of finding an exact criterion for the distinction between L1 and L2, they suggest that 'one could say arbitrarily that any language learnt by the child before the age of instruction, from parents, from others, such as a nurse, looking after it, or from other children, is an L1.'

What underlies the native–foreign or L1–L2 distinction, then, is first of all the assumed importance of an unbroken oral tradition. But some attach great importance to the order of learning and insist that 'native' means 'first-learnt' in the most literal sense – for instance, even in those cases where a person has partially or completely forgotten his first language through long disuse. The point that is emphasized by those who hold this view is lack of interference from other languages. A second-learnt language will often be learnt at least in part through books; but even if it is learnt entirely through the ear, the learner's mind when he starts learning the language will no longer be a *tabula rasa*, and it is presumed that there will be some influence, however slight, from the first on any later-learnt language.

Even in the exceptional case where no trace of this interference is noticeable, it is rather the result of removal of something once present than of its never having been there. This therefore casts a shadow of possible lack of authenticity – of possible deviation from native tradition – on any but the first language (Hughes, 1962, p. 20).

In this extreme form it is easy to find fault with the distinction. In the first place, it is not always easy to identify a person's first language, with certainty. Or rather, one wonders how literally to interpret the term 'first'. For instance, during a short period – a few months perhaps – before learning his parents' language, a child may use the language of a foreign nursemaid or of playmates in a foreign country (see p. 51), though later on this language may vanish completely from his conscious mind. Are we to regard a language like that as his 'native' language? If not, what is the maximum period of time that we are allowed to disregard in cases of this kind, and why? Any decision in this matter, short of a literal interpretation must be arbitrary; but a literal interpretation will often be absurd. How confused, in fact, our thinking (or the terms we use) about these matters can be is illustrated by a remark by Lado (1964, p. 37) in a chapter dealing with second-language learning. He proposes to exclude from consideration, he says, cases of second-language learning by young children in which the learning goes 'beyond the level of mastery of the first language, as at that level it would become the first language.' One suspects that he is here using 'first' in two different senses in the same sentence.

Secondly, it must not be forgotten that even a first language is acquired by trial and error. Despite the hypothesized innate capacity for language learning (section 17) with its concomitant theory that early child language is only in part an imitation of adult syntax (e.g. McNeill, 1970), it remains true to say that a child's acquistion of his mother tongue is by no means an automatic process. Over a number of years he has a great many shots at the right sounds and grammar before he succeeds in mastering the language. No one learns his first language, therefore, without going through that process of which Hughes is so suspicious and which he describes as 'removal of something once present'.

Thirdly, while undoubtedly a first-learnt language tends to

influence a second-learnt (though a great deal can be done by good teachers to reduce this interference), it is equally true that there is influence the other way, from a second on a first language. If the second language has greater social prestige, conscious efforts will probably be made to keep it pure, while no special care will be devoted to the first, little-regarded language. Obvious instances are immigrant languages in the United States, which are learnt, if at all, as first languages, but often in a form that makes a resident of the European country of origin smile (Mencken, 1941, pp. 616–97). Since some second-language learning is part of the training of practically all educated people in the western world, it follows that there is no such thing as a 'pure' tradition of educated speech in the mother tongue. The influence of the school languages, Latin and French, on Western European languages is indeed too well-known to need demonstration, though it should perhaps be pointed out that this influence is felt not only in vocabulary, phraseology and syntax but even in phonemic structure, as witness the development of the /f/v/w/ distinction in Middle English (Pyles, 1971, pp. 62–3).

Finally, although a small child acquires his speech before he learns to read and write, any educated adult's knowledge of his first language – even in its simplest spoken form as he would use it to a child – is so permeated by features of the written language that any talk of a 'pure' oral tradition becomes absurd. For instance, but for the existence of the written language, 'you was' and double negatives would probably still be normal English usage (Leonard, 1962). What the child learns, therefore, after a good deal of correction, is something which is not without 'a shadow of possible lack of authenticity' as Hughes understands this term. Purity does not exist.

It is interesting to speculate on the reason why the chimera of purity is pursued with such zeal, or such pedantry. In the first place, there is probably some link with a view which is widely, though not universally, held among linguists, that speech is primary in relation to writing and hence supposedly purer. But this in its turn can be traced to nineteenth-century

Romantic ideas about the 'folk' and the genuineness of the folk tradition in this as in other fields. Hence the supposed naturalness of folk speech as opposed to the 'artificiality' of the standard language. These ideas, foreshadowed centuries ago by Dante (see section 13), came to the fore in the nineteenth century under the influence of Romantic nationalism. They are reflected, for instance, in the efforts made in some countries to weed out words of foreign origin and substitute something 'purer', and in a tendency to look upon speech as more natural than writing, less inhibited by artificial restraints imposed from outside, such as rules derived from Latin grammar.

Another contributory cause is the idea, prevalent until recently, that the mother tongue is a divine gift (see section 12) bestowed upon us in infancy when heaven lies about us, and forming part of that sacred trust, our national heritage. A gift like that imposes a sacred obligation to cherish it, to see that it is not tampered with and, in particular, to see that it is not adulterated by admixture from foreign sources.

Curiously enough, the idea that the mother tongue is unique and inviolable finds support from an unexpected quarter. A scientist must never tamper with his material, and since linguists aim at being scientific they must follow the same procedure. The 'native' language is thought to be entirely spontaneous, unless indeed it is messed about with by pedantic grammarians; it is viewed in almost the same light as man's physiological processes, over which he has no control and of which he is only vaguely aware. Hence the conclusion is drawn that it is primarily the 'native' language that a linguist should study. And so we find Romantics and scientists joining hands in defence of the uniqueness and inviolability of the mother tongue.

Is the scientific position in this matter sound? As pointed out earlier, first-language learning is not an entirely automatic process; it involves a good deal of trial and error. Nor is the mother tongue necessarily purer than a second-learnt language; it is open to external influences from other languages and from the written form of the language. There remains the point that the mother tongue is usually, though not invariably, learnt at a time when there is no knowledge of any other language in the learner's mind; but it is not clear that this fact has any necessary or permanent influence upon subsequent language performance, serving to distinguish it from second-language performance. What characterizes the mother tongue, the primary language as compared with a secondary language, is the user's feeling of intimacy in relation to it, of being at home in it, of it being part of him as a person. But this is a product of long exposure and regular use and as such is attainable, given suitable conditions, in a second language.

It appears, then, that the basis for making a sharp distinction between a 'native' and a second language is rather shaky. Moreover, definitions vary. If oral transmission is emphasized, a person may have several 'native' languages; if chronology, he may have none – in the sense that he may have forgotten his first language, which may never have survived beyond early childhood. What purpose, in that case, does the distinction serve? It records a historical fact – namely, priority of learning or learning by oral transmission – which may or may not be significant. In the majority of cases, it is true, this fact or its absence is reflected in subsequent language performance; but this is not so in all cases, and there seems to be nothing inevitable about it. The situation may merely reflect the poor quality of much second-language instruction and amount to a corroboration of the view that a direct type of teaching is the best.

The difficulty of operating with the terms 'native' and 'L1' is illustrated by a passage in Halliday, McIntosh and Strevens (1964, p. 224), in which it appears to the present writer that the use of 'L1' conflicts with the definition given earlier on by the same authors and quoted on p. 55 of this book:

In general, 'native language' equals 'L1'; that is, the majority of people have one native language which is, and remains throughout their lives, the one from which all their registers and restricted languages are drawn. A minority of people have more than one native language; and a minority – not the same minority – replace the native language by a foreign language as their L1. A few even acquire more than one language as L1: that is, they come to use more than one language for all the purposes for which they use any language.

In view of this state of affairs, it is natural to ask whether it is advisable to continue to use terms of this kind in writing that aims at scientific accuracy. The situation is further confused by the fact that 'native' happens to be used by laymen in ways that conflict with either of the definitions mentioned above. Professor O'Doherty of University College, Dublin, says (1958, p. 284)

for the benefit of our visitors, I should explain that the words 'native language' or 'mother tongue' are conventionally used here [in Ireland] by many of our people to refer to the ancestral language rather than to the language of the primary society into which the child is born. This is a simple fact of linguistic usage which has had far-reaching effects on the thinking of many of our people with regard to the problem of bilingualism.

An illustration of this usage is found in the American critic Harry Levin's statement (1948, p. 15): 'That English was not Joyce's native language, in the strictest sense, he was keenly aware.' It is probably also this idea that underlies Stephen Dedalus' reflection on English, his first-learnt language: 'This language, so familiar and so foreign, will always be for me an acquired speech' (Joyce, 1916, p. 221).

Finally, we also sometimes find the word used in contexts where the meaning seems to be, or verge upon, 'having the language as one's best, one's primary medium': 'the reader (or listener) has to be almost a native speaker in order to appreciate the full implications of a joke' (Hall, 1959, pp. 124–5). Or: 'many Indians are native English-speakers, or nearly so; if English is not the language in which they lisp their first words, it is still acquired very early' (Wain, 1961, p. 7).

The complexity of the situation makes it difficult to suggest a simple and unambiguous terminology. 'L1' and 'L2' seem clear and simple, but chronology and oral transmission may not be the most significant, let alone the only significant, factors. Language dominance, too, ought certainly to be indicated, as originally intended by Catford (see p. 55). One way of doing this would be to add the letters A and B, as in LA2 ('dominant second-learnt language') and LB1 ('second-dary first-learnt language'). Even this, however, is an over-simplification (Christophersen, 1964, p. 22–3); for instance, it begs the tricky question of what constitutes a language as distinct from a dialect. Is a German–Swiss (*Schwyzertütsch*) speaker using a second language when he writes in Standard German (see p. 32). Not infrequently, differences in speech wide enough to justify classification as separate languages are concealed by the use of a common written standard. Moreover, dominance is not a simple matter; among other things, it will not necessarily remain constant throughout a person's life. This will be further discussed in the next chapter.

Four **Bilingualism**

22 Kinds and degrees

There was a time when bilingualism was looked upon as a freak and was regarded with something of that feeling of awe and half-incredulous curiosity that we tend to have about, say, Siamese twins. It was a condition that was thought to exist in those relatively few cases where two languages are started at exactly the same time, in early childhood. In such cases, it was thought, the two languages would be completely in balance, in the sense that the individual would be able later on to use either of them with the same ease in any situation. This belief was linked with certain ideas, discussed in the preceding chapter, about the mother tongue as something unique which could never be equalled by any later-learnt language; a bilingual person, it was thought, was simply one who had two mother tongues.

Bilingualism is in fact a far more complex phenomenon; there are different kinds and degrees of it, and age of learning is only one of many variable factors. The languages are by no means always in balance; there is often some degree of specialization, and usually one of the languages will be found to be dominant in relation to the other, will be more the person's 'own' language. Most important of all, perhaps, bilingualism is far more wide spread nowadays than many people imagine. Moreover, in years to come, as a result of easier communication, closer international contacts and, perhaps, more efficient language teaching, bilingualism is likely to increase by leaps and bounds.

The term 'bilingualism' means 'the possession of two languages'. There is also a term 'multilingualism', 'the possession of several languages', but most observations regarding bilingualism are true, *mutatis mutandis*, of multilingualism as well. Strictly, bilingualism can be used as a description of a nation as well as an individual, but these two types of bilingualism must be kept apart. In theory one could imagine a nation, or at least a political unit, consisting of two mother-tongue groups none of whose members was personally bilingual. In practice, however, if there is to be effective communication between the two groups in a bilingual country, some of the members at least will have to be personally bilingual. The following discussion will be mostly concerned with personal bilingualism.

It was once customary to define personal bilingualism, as Bloomfield did (1935, p. 56), as 'native-like control of two languages'. For various reasons, including the fact that 'native-like' is not a very precise term (see p. 53), this definition has now been abandoned by linguists, who no longer presume to specify how much a person needs to know of each language to be regarded as bilingual. The knowledge may vary from a mere smattering to literary mastery (Haugen, 1956, p. 10). While the degree of proficiency is thus disregarded in defining bilingualism, many would emphasize instead the habitual use of two languages as a necessary condition. But this definition, too, must not be pressed too far; nobody would undertake to lay down the precise degree of frequency that is implied in the word 'habitual'.

Age of learning, as was said earlier, is not included in the definition of bilingualism, but we can distinguish between different kinds of bilingualism – infant, child, adolescent and adult – according to the stage in a bilingual person's life at which he acquired his two languages or the second of the two. Another criterion for differentiation is the place or places where the languages are habitually used. Thus we have home bilingualism where different members of the same family make use of different languages, and we have home–school or home–work bilingualism if the home and the school – or the place of work – differ in the languages they use.

Another distinction that has to be borne in mind in talking

about bilingualism is between an all-purpose and a specialized knowledge of a language (see p. 29). A bilingual person's command of one of his languages may be very specialized in the sense of being mostly confined to a fairly narrow aspect of life, for instance some technical knowledge or skill. Or it may be specialized in the sense of being confined to either the spoken or the written form. It is not uncommon for a bilingual person to be literate, or truly literate, in only one of his languages.

A distinction which many linguists recognize is between so-called coordinate and compound bilingualism, (Weinreich, 1953; Haugen, 1956; Macnamara, in Alatis, 1970). The terms have been criticized as ill-defined, and doubts have been thrown on the value of the distinction; but although pure cases probably do not exist, the terms serve to indicate certain tendencies. In coordinate bilingualism, the two languages function independently and express two distinct backgrounds and ways of life, two cultures. In compound bilingualism both languages serve to express the same background, the same culture, as for instance in home bilingualism. Compound bilingualism invariably affects the two languages: there will be interference in the sense of mutual influence between them. As a result they become parallel means of expression; translation between them becomes easy and, as somebody said, rather paradoxically, they become in effect one language with two modes of expression. In practice we find, not two groups, but a great many gradations between the two extremes. Two languages used in the same home obviously express, in anything that relates to the home, the same culture; but two languages in the same country could express different cultures. The latter is most often the case in bilingual countries and is often the cause of some friction. Even so, the fact of living together within the same political boundaries may give two groups of people a body of shared culture – leisure habits, social stratification, events in history, etc. – which will make communication easier. According to Deutsch (1953, p. 71), this fact enables a Swiss to communicate more effectively with another Swiss speaking a different language from his own than with a speaker of his own language belonging to another country. The shared culture between two language groups in a case like this will be reflected to some extent in their linguistic usage; the two languages will draw nearer to each other.

The latter tendency may cause difficulty in cases where there is also, for one or both languages, a unilingual hinterland, another country in which that language is used as the only language. Usually in a case like that the bilingual country will regard itself as peripheral in relation to the hinterland and will look to the latter for its standard form of the language, especially in writing. Now a standard language is *eo ipso* a model of behaviour, and for two nations to share a model of behaviour means either some mutual adjustment or the acceptance by one nation of some of the ways of the other. The latter is usually the case in a bilingual country in relation to the hinterland, at least where the written language is concerned. In this way, a wide divergence may arise between speech and writing in the bilingual country (Graham, 1956).

In some cases several nations share a literary standard but retain their separate vernacular forms of the spoken language. We thus get a kind of bilingualism for which Ferguson in 1959 coined the term 'diglossia'; it exists, for instance, in the German-speaking world and in Switzerland in particular (see pp. 32 and 61). It appears to depend on a state of equilibrium between the feeling of cohesion, which supports the standard, and local patriotism, which keeps the vernacular in being. Since there is no essential difference between two dialects and two languages, Fishman (1967; 1970) has more recently extended the term 'diglossia' to apply to any community which regularly used two language varieties (dialects or languages), each with its well-defined sphere of use. For the individual citizen it means that some of his social roles (e.g. husband, father, friend) are performed in one medium, and others (e.g. employer, member of a profession, member of a church) in another. The two languages taken together have the full range of functions for the bilingual that a single language has for a unilingual person.

The essential thing about diglossia is thus that the two languages or dialects are in balance and do not compete, and there are consequently no major conflicts. How many situations of this kind exist in the world is not clear; a bilingual situation tends to be unstable and to give rise to tensions. Certainly the bilingual problems that are found in many parts belong chiefly to situations where the languages compete, where there is no widely accepted social consensus as to which language is to be used in what circumstances, and where consequently the individual is faced with a choice. Second-language learning is likely to give rise to a situation of the latter kind.

What has been said, here and elsewhere in this book, about language and culture may be represented a little more schematically. It has been pointed out before (see especially section 8) that there is a close link between language and culture; it follows that bilingualism and biculturalism are closely related phenomena. In theory there are four possible combinations:

(a) unilingualism – uniculturalism;
(b) unilingualism – biculturalism;
(c) bilingualism – uniculturalism;
(d) bilingualism – biculturalism.

The first does not concern us here. The second is of considerable interest: can the same language serve to express two different cultures? The answer appears to be that it depends on what we understand by 'the same language', and this is ultimately an arbitrary decision (Halliday, McIntosh and Strevens, 1964, pp. 76–7). To the extent that two cultures differ, the linguistic media that are used to express them will also differ (p. 25), irrespective of whether we choose to call them regional variants, dialects or separate languages. The third combination is identical with what has been called compound bilingualism; in its pure form this is extremely rare. The fourth combination is what has been called coordinate bilingualism; again the pure-bred variety may be rare, but something of this kind is common wherever two languages are used by the same individual or the same nation without a clear division of labour between them. It gives rise to various psychological and sociological problems, which will be discussed in subsequent sections.

23 Dominance

Is it conceivable that an individual could ever have an exactly equal command of two languages? The answer depends on how strictly we interpret the word 'equal'. The technical term for absolute equality is equilingualism or ambilingualism (Morrison, 1958; Catford, 1959). Occasionally, no doubt, we may discover a case that approximates very closely to ambilingualism; but in the strictest sense of the word, and particularly if we add the proviso that the command of each language must be 'native-like', must be indistinguishable from that of a unilingual user of the language, the type can be seen to have no existence. It is interesting, however, to speculate on what it would involve. The whole of such a person's experience from birth up, whether at home, at school, at work or at play, would have had to be duplicated or rather experienced equally greatly and contemporaneously through the two languages. Even other languages which such a person may happen to know would be related equally greatly – or equally little – to his two languages. For instance, a French–English ambilingual studying Latin would have to develop two pronunciations of Latin, French–Latin and English–Latin. If he is interested in sailing or in collecting butterflies or playing in a band, these activities would have to be associated equally with both languages; but this will be difficult if the relevant literature is mostly in one of them, or if the people with whom he shares these interests belong mostly to one community. And so on and so forth. In practice, the demand for absolute equality could never be fulfilled

This is not to say that it is impossible to know two languages 'like a native' – if we interpret that phrase a little vaguely and perhaps rather generously, bearing in mind the difficulties mentioned in section 20. What it means is that it is impossible for the command of two languages to be exactly equal, since they cannot cover exactly the same area of experience. Thus there will often be some sort of specialization; each language will be associated with particular interests and activities – or just a particular group of people. On the other hand, if we interpret ambilingualism to mean merely 'balanced bilingualism' – that is, approximately but not absolutely equal command of two languages – undoubtedly the phenomenon exists.

Is it possible to measure a bilingual's relative skill in his two languages and thus determine which of his languages is dominant? This kind of measurement is difficult because much more is involved than mere fluency, accent and size of vocabulary (Weinreich, 1953, pp. 74–80; Haugen, 1956, pp. 73–8; Macnamara, 1966, pp. 9–38; 1967, pp. 61–4; Fishman, 1968, pp. 24–6; Kelly, 1969, pp. 79–119, 191–239). The mode of use (speech or writing; formal or informal) and the place of operation (home, work, or church, etc.) would have to be given weight, but how much weight? Clearly it is important to know which language is used in the speaker's intimate daily life, and there would be a great deal of point in regarding that language as dominant. But suppose the speaker is an ambitious man and has a much wider general command of another language, which he considers more important because it carries greater social prestige or greater chances of promotion in his professional career? Emotional involvement is obviously an important factor, but a person may be emotionally involved in different ways with different languages.

Any measurement of language dominance, therefore, must of necessity incorporate arbitrary decisions with regard to weighting. Moreover, it is important to realize that the result is valid only at the particular moment when the measurement is carried out. Where a person's two languages are almost in balance, the equilibrium may be upset either by external factors, such as a removal to different surroundings, or by psychological factors, such as a change of sympathies and a consequent shift of language loyalty.

Without a clear definition of dominance it is obviously difficult to demonstrate that a shift of dominance has occurred in an individual person's life. Even the preservation of a foreign accent does not necessarily rule out dominance. What can be demonstrated, however, is a shift in a bilingual person's use of his two languages. Many immigrant parents after a while abandon their first language, at least for most purposes, and their children will sometimes completely abandon the language of their early childhood for that which they learn in school and which most or all of their friends speak. Sometimes no trace of the earlier language survives in the person's conscious mind (Haugen, 1956, p. 74), and he ceases to be bilingual. For reasons of social advancement, children of immigrants often make conscious efforts to dissociate themselves from their foreign home background. In the same way, in many countries, children from homes where the parents speak a dialect will abandon this for the standard language if their education leads them to associate themselves with speakers of the standard.

It is sometimes argued that a person's first-learnt language, even if partly forgotten, will still remain closer to his heart. This is a difficult matter to investigate, since for obvious reasons sentiments are not easy to measure objectively. It is interesting, however, to note what happens if a bilingual person is afflicted with aphasia (loss of language through brain injury or disease). If the bilingual's two languages are more or less in balance before aphasia occurs, will they be affected equally? As a rule both languages are affected, but there is often a time-lag between them, both in their disappearance and, where a cure is effected, in their reappearance (Goldstein, 1948, pp. 138–46; Weinreich, 1953, p. 76, pp. 77–8; Osgood and Miron, 1963, pp. 35–6; Geschwind, in Millikan and Darley, 1967, pp. 197–8). It was believed for a long time that the first-learnt language would invariably be more tenacious, the last to disappear and the first to reappear, but clinical experience does not support this view. In many cases the order is reversed, or only the second-learnt language is recovered. A significant factor influencing the early recovery of a language appears to be its more frequent use and greater familiarity immediately before the person became aphasic. Another and perhaps more important factor is emotional involvement: the second-learnt language may have come, for one reason or another, to have stronger emotional associations – for instance, by long and happy residence in a community where that language is spoken, by friendships, love affairs, etc., creating a degree of emotional dependence and leading the person to identify himself with the speakers of the second-learnt language and to consider himself a member of their community. Very often, no doubt, the two factors are operative together.

Since language dominance is not a constant, there might conceivably be cases where a shift occurs several times in the course of a person's life. Owing to the close link between language, personality and community, however, this seems unlikely, though perhaps not impossible. On the other hand, a second-learnt language which for a time has been brought to something like 'perfection' (see p. 53), but not dominance, has been known to deteriorate later on through disuse. In cases of senile decay, 'second childhood', it may happen that a forgotten language returns to the conscious mind, presumably by some process which could be explained in terms of Penfield's theory (section 18).

24 The creation of bilinguals

Since neither age of learning nor degree of proficiency is part of the definition of bilingualism, it follows that anybody who has learnt enough of a foreign language to use it regularly for some purpose or other – for example, showing overseas visitors over a museum, or reading technical literature in his field of specialization – must be considered bilingual, if only in some small degree. As some have pointed out (Catford, 1959; Fishman, 1966b), foreign-language teaching is a process of creating bilinguals. Moreover, despite all assertions to the contrary (see sections 20–21) it seems clear that, given the will, the opportunity and the right approach, there is no limit to the degree of proficiency that may be achieved in a second-learnt language. As Halliday, McIntosh and Strevens say (1964, p. 78), not all ambilinguals – the word is obviously used by them in the sense of 'balanced bilinguals' (see p. 68) –

have learnt both their languages as L1s, that is, before the age of instruction.

This last observation is of considerable interest to those who plan second-language courses for people seeking an all-purpose command. If we were to attempt a definition of fully successful second-language teaching, it would presumably be something like this: teaching of such a kind and quality that it turns good pupils into balanced bilinguals. Some may not consider this a desirable goal, but that is a separate issue which will be discussed in a different context (see section 29). Or they may consider it an 'unrealistic' goal; but in that case they have to account for the admittedly small but not insignificant number of successful learners. If it be objected that such cases are too few to allow any valid conclusions to be drawn, it is salutary to reflect that cases of people who fully understand, say, the theory of radioactivity are exceedingly few when compared with the general mass of humanity. But nobody assumes from this that they are abnormal and that all the rest of humanity would be incapable of learning if properly instructed. Expansion or improvement of teaching, whether of physics or languages, means an attempt to change the existing state of affairs.

If now we turn our attention to cases in which a balanced form of bilingualism has in fact been achieved, and at least in part through formal instruction, we may be able to discover the underlying mental processes. What distinguishes these people psychologically from unsuccessful learners? The theory that Lambert and his associates have evolved (Lambert, 1963; Lambert *et al.*, 1968; Gardner, 1966) is that the most successful learning is achieved by students who have what Lambert calls an integrative motivation, a desire to model themselves on valued members of the target community and a willingness to consider themselves, in a sense, members of that community (see section 7). This kind of language learning involves much more than acquisition of a new set of verbal habits or rules; the student must adopt subtle features of behaviour and attitude which belong to the new community. To do this he must obviously be favourably disposed towards that community and have an interest in learning their language in order to understand more about them. A typical formulation of his purpose would be, 'I think French will help me better to understand the French-Canadian people and their way of life' (Gardner, 1966, p. 28).

Interesting confirmation of what has just been said is found in the memoirs of Ernest Dimnet, a Frenchman who came to prefer English to French as his literary medium: 'I have often reflected on the curious osmose which carries the psychology of a nation into the soul of a man not belonging to it, through the medium of the language. Perhaps, having in early middle life changed my literary expression from French to English, I have had an exceptional chance to collect observations on that phenomenon' (1935, p. 194). For adults learning a foreign language from necessity, he says, there tends to be a veil between them and the messages they receive. 'Not so when a language is studied from curiosity about the people who speak it. . . . I learned English in that way through sympathetic curiosity enhanced by intercourse with men I wished in many ways to resemble' (p. 195).

It was pointed out earlier that there is probably a link between personality disposition and ability to learn languages. Difficulties in acquiring a good pronunciation sometimes turn out to be due to a feeling by the student that the attempt to make him change his speech habits is an attack upon his personality, his identity as a person (Abercrombie, 1956, p. 6). And so in a sense it is. It is not so much that there is any encroachment on his original personality; it is truer to say that something is being added, an extra personality or dimension to his personality, an extra mode of behaviour. He is on the way to becoming bilingual and bicultural.

The observation that there seems to be a link between personality and capacity for second-language learning in the individual prompts the question whether the same could be true of nations. Nations, too, have personalities in the sense of a tendency for each nation to conform to a certain type – not as formerly believed, genetically determined, but the product of learning, part of the national tradition (see section 8).

Now some national temperaments are probably more authoritarian than others, and some nations are popularly thought to be less good at learning languages than others. Could there be a link? Conceivably; but we need to know a great deal more before we can decide. Other factors, such as relative size, seem to be involved; the bigger a nation is, the less obvious will seem the need for learning another nation's language. On the other hand, we may be reasoning in a circle, since size itself could be a determining factor in the formation of the national personality.

25 Pains and pleasures of bilingualism

Bilinguals and bilingualism have often in the past been looked upon with unfriendly eyes. This, no doubt, is the reason why bilingual people seldom go out of their way to advertise their bilingualism; sometimes they deliberately suppress the fact that they are bilingual in the hope of passing for ordinary members of the social group that they prefer to belong to. Many try to get away from the circumstances that forced bilingualism on them in order to plunge into unilingualism in the language of their preference (see p. 69). Sometimes they succeed almost too well, as in the case reported by Nida (1958) of the son of immigrants to America who tried so hard and so successfully to become identified with the prestige-possessing English-speaking community that later on, when he went out as a missionary to the Middle East, he was unable to learn the local language. What are the reasons for this hostility to bilinguals and bilingualism?

A number of half-truths and misconceptions about bilingualism are common currency, or were until recently, in wide circles. Jespersen (1922, p. 148) said that a bilingual child hardly learns either of his languages as perfectly as he would have done if he had limited himself to one. He thought, too, that the brain effort required to master two languages instead of one must surely hamper the child's learning of other subjects. More curiously, he thought that no bilingual child had ever developed into a great poet, and he quoted with applause Schuchardt's saying that a bilingual man has two strings to his bow, both rather slack. There seems an echo here of Sweet's surprising statement (1899, p. 82): 'No phenomenal linguist has ever produced real literature, nor, what is more remarkable, ever made any great contribution to the science of language.'

In the light of present-day knowledge, these views can be seen to suffer from varying degrees of distortion. The first part of Sweet's contention is plainly false (see p. 77), and the second part may have been true in Sweet's time but is certainly not so now – which perhaps accounts for our greater understanding of the problem of bilingualism. But all these views are mild compared with some of the allegations that have been made by others. 'If one were to believe such writers as Weisgerber, bilingualism is capable of impairing the intelligence of a whole ethnic group and crippling its creative abilities for generations' (Weinreich, 1953, p. 116). Is there any scientific evidence to support such a view?

Child bilingualism most often occurs where children from a linguistic minority receive their school instruction in the state language. A common contention is that this retards their education, and that their knowledge of the home language suffers. Owing to the difficulty of measuring bilingualism (see section 23) it is almost impossible to give an authoritative judgement in this matter. A particular difficulty is that of finding comparable groups of children, unilingual and bilingual, differing only in the one factor to be measured. Very often it turns out that there are significant differences in their social and economic backgrounds as well, which may affect the score.

Nevertheless, it is fairly commonly admitted by unbiased investigators that bilingual schoolchildren are most often behind their unilingual contemporaries in language skills (reading, spelling, etc.) in both their languages during at least part of their school career (Haugen, 1956, pp. 82–4, 112–15; Macnamara, 1966, chapter 3). It seems, however, that the 'bilingual handicap' – which is never more than a year or two – often diminishes with age, and by the time a student reaches college or university level his performance in the second language – the language of instruction – will be fully equal to that of unilingual students. His performance in the home language is likely by this time to vary considerably from home to home, and it will most probably fall below that in the second language because it will be restricted to a narrower range of experience. There is some evidence – but like so much evidence in these matters it has not gone unchallenged (Macnamara, 1966, p. 22) – that if both languages are used side by side as media of instruction and if the climate of opinion is equally favourable to both, there need be no language handicap.

The contention that child bilingualism impairs the intelligence has often been made but never satisfactorily proved or disproved owing to the difficulty of excluding extraneous factors from the experiments. There is a good deal of evidence against this view, and W. R. Jones (1960, p. 71) concludes that 'bilingualism need not be a source of intellectual disadvantage'. In a test in Montreal a few years ago Elizabeth Peal and W. E. Lambert (1962) found that a group of truly bilingual ten-year-old children from French-speaking homes did significantly better than a unilingual control group in both intelligence and language tests. What the experimenters were unable to determine was whether the children were bilingual because they were intelligent, or vice versa, but they suggested that intelligent children might see more clearly the advantage of knowing English as well as French.

In those cases where a language is started as a school subject and then later, perhaps in early manhood, brought to a degree of proficiency that equals or excels the first language, there can obviously be no question of impairment of the intelligence. On the other hand, the intense concentration on the second-learnt language may have some slightly adverse effect on the command of the first; but the person will nearly always in such a case feel that he could restore the balance if he wished and if circumstances made that desirable.

A feature of the language performance of all bilinguals is the possibility of 'interference' as it is commonly called, influence from one language upon the other (Weinreich, 1953, chapter 2;

Haugen, 1956, pp. 50–55). It is perhaps this that underlies the critical attitude of many people to bilingualism: they fear that the 'purity' of the language, either language, is in danger. Purity is an ideal with a doubtful theoretical basis (see p. 57); in practice, what people object to is any deviation from the existing norm for unilingual people, however 'impure' that norm may be historically. Interference can in fact range all the way from the grossest foreign accent to the occasional use of a word or idiom imported from, or influenced in its use by, the other language. The cause can be poor quality teaching of the second language, or it can be a difference in cultural background from the unilingual hinterland (p. 65). It can also be laziness, the line of least resistance, especially among speakers of a minority language, which is particularly open to outside influence, or it could be simply a slip of the tongue due to confusion, momentary or permanent.

On a balanced view there seems nothing alarming in this; most educated bilingual adults are aware of the difficulty and manage to keep at least the language of their preference close to the norm. The feeling exists among many that if they were in a position to drop the other language and let it fade out of their consciousness, their command of the remaining one would be in every respect like that of unilinguals.

It would be useless, nevertheless, to deny that unconscious deviations from the norm occur in the usage of many bilinguals, at least in their less good language. Foreigners' mistakes are a common source of amusement – so common in fact that this has led to mistaken ideas about their inevitability (see section 20). Even when the grammar and most normal idioms have been mastered, quaintnesses like 'old Britain' – intended as an emotionally coloured phrase similar to 'old England' – are likely to occur. On the other hand, it should not be forgotten that so-called 'native' speakers often have surprising lacunae in their knowledge of the language, and yet we react differently to these. We may be amused: 'Fancy not knowing that!' But we let the mistake pass because, 'After all, it is his own language!' With a foreigner, the expectation that sooner or later he is going to slip up sometimes leads to the presumption of mistakes which do not exist. In a review of a book by a Frenchman dealing with George Borrow's style, Professor G. Tillotson suggested that the author's feeling for English was defective: 'Is "disembogue" an unusual word in English? No – it occurs as often as the thing it denotes is referred to' (1959, pp. 266–7).

Considering the relatively small number of fairly balanced bilinguals in the world compared with unilingual people and people with only a smattering of another language, it is a matter for wonder, *pace* Sweet and Jespersen, that there are or have been so many writers of distinction among them. Conrad, the most frequently quoted name, is interesting because of the late development of his second-learnt language, but since he confined his creative writing to that language alone, he was not bilingual as a writer. Throughout the ages, however, there have been people writing with distinction, some in prose and some in verse, in more than one language (Forster, 1961; 1970); in some cases each language belongs to a particular period in the writer's life. Among the better known of those using English as one of their media may be mentioned John Gower, Charles d'Orléans, Milton, Tagore, Samuel Beckett, Karen Blixen, Arthur Koestler and Nabokov. This is not to say that producing imaginative literature of a high order in two languages is an easy matter (Haugen, 1956, p. 70). Most people will probably feel that that kind of command can only be reached and sustained, if at all, in one language at a time – not necessarily, of course, the language they learnt in the cradle.

The feeling that many people have that there is something unnatural about bilingualism in the abstract is equally strong in regard to individual bilingual people whom they may meet. Coordinate bilinguals have a kind of double or divided allegiance; they belong in a sense to two communities, and it is this divided allegiance that strikes unilingual people as 'startling, abnormal, almost uncanny' (Martinet, in Weinreich, 1953, p. vii). Some people have a feeling, when talking to a person whom they know to be bilingual, that they cannot fully trust him and confide in him because, after all,

'He is not one of us.' It is true that on the surface he may seem to be 'one of us', but then 'That is precisely the trouble: he is not what he seems to be.' This suspicion may exist in both communities, thus making the bilingual a 'marginal man'. It is the main reason why many bilinguals would like to get away from their bilingualism in order to become fully integrated members of the community of their preference.

Is this supposed unreliability of bilinguals all imaginary: is it all in the observer, or has it a basis in reality? To some extent it is in the observer; it is a fear of strangers. It only arises in cases where the bilingual's other allegiance is to a community the observer does not know well and is inclined to dislike or distrust. Somebody who is bilingual in a dialect and in the standard language is usually fully acceptable, because the allegiance to the dialect community is subsumed under the national allegiance. Somebody who belongs to a linguistic minority is rather less acceptable to the majority group, and where the other allegiance is to a foreign community, suspicion is likely to arise. It seems unnatural to most of us that a person should have two modes of behaviour belonging to two quite separate communities of people. Which, we ask, is his own way? Or has he not got a way that he can call his own?

It is useful in this connection to remind ourselves that we all vary our behaviour and our mode of speech to suit our surroundings. As Alistair Reid says (1963, p. 30):

Moving between several languages . . . only dramatizes what happens all the time within our own language: whatever our accent, we do not speak in the same voice to a baby, to a clergyman, to an old friend, to a foreigner. . . . If voices are anything to go by, then the idea of having a fixed, firm self is wildly illusory. We expect those with whom we are in sympathy to listen to what is behind our voice; it is horrifying to have someone listen to nothing more than what we say.

The difficulty with a bilingual is that some of his roles are performed in a mode of speech which is beyond our comprehension, and so our suspicion is aroused.

Still, the feeling of dislike and distrust is not entirely without some basis in reality. It has to be recognized that there is more maladjustment among bilinguals than among unilingual people. The strain on somebody belonging, and yet not fully belonging, to two communities, the conflicts of behaviour and the stigma of inferiority that this situation may involve, may well bring out undesirable personality traits. It should be emphasized that this emotional maladjustment is environmentally determined and is not the result of any strain caused by having to cope with two languages. The bilingual's difficulties are almost entirely extralinguistic. As Fishman says (1966a, p. 371), talking of American conditions, 'the bilingualism of hundreds of thousands of Americans is a liability in their lives, and this for no reason inherent in the nature of bilingualism *per se*. It is our treatment of bilinguals and of bilingualism that brings this sad state of affairs into being.'

Even an emotionally balanced bilingual, secure in his membership of two communities, is likely to feel a certain conflict or strain at times in having to reconcile or choose between two modes of conduct (Haugen, 1956, p. 84). He will feel to some extent, but only to some extent, as if he were two different people according to his surroundings. It is this necessity for personality adjustment that has sometimes been dramatized into a split personality, a point of view which is strongly criticized by Elwert (1959, pp. 342–4). Still, the testimony of many practising bilinguals cannot be lightly dismissed. Rather surprisingly, culturally related communities will sometimes differ markedly – and perhaps clash – in their systems of values within certain areas, such as games, culinary taste, drinking habits, etc., and even in matters involving some moral judgement such as attitude to animals or matrimonial fidelity. Religion is another area where there may be a clash. A bilingual may find himself under the necessity of either liking – or pretending to like – in one community what he dislikes in another or standing out as an eccentric in one of his communities with the risk of being rejected.

It is important to emphasize once more that the difficulties of adjustment that a bilingual person may experience are the result of his two cultures rather than his languages. Precisely the same difficulties may arise in cases where language is not involved as a factor, as illustrated by the following personal confession (Hamilton, 1963, p. 76): 'To be Anglo-Irish is not conducive to a sense of stability, in that to belong to two countries is to belong that much the less to each. It means, in the republic of Eire, to be to some degree an outsider – the spectator of a regime in which as a citizen of Britain one has no part; in England, to be at a distance from – not wholly identified with – one's fellows; to be conscious – and proud, too – of one's Irish origins; quick to take up the challenge for Ireland; resentful perhaps of that faintly patronizing tone the English can adopt regarding any people other than themselves.' The same detachment may be found among bilinguals. A Welsh–English bilingual has confessed that among English people he feels he is Welsh and among Welsh people English.

Since language teaching means creating bilinguals (see section 24), the difficulties of bilingualism have a direct relevance for anybody concerned with either theory or practice in this field of activity. Is there a danger, as Carroll once hinted (see section 2), that foreign-language teaching may one day become so efficient that it leads to some of the personal difficulties just mentioned? The answer is that it has already done so in some cases; and any bilingual person is likely to experience some of the difficulties mentioned. Although Shaw's Eliza Doolittle is an imaginary character, and although Shaw grossly underestimated the length of time required for the transformation process, the idea of the play is by no means fantastic, and the consequences could well be more serious than Shaw imagined. Once a shift of dominance has occurred, it cannot easily be undone.

Others besides Carroll are aware of these difficulties and the likelihood of their occurrence among language learners. The term *anomie* has been used to describe the feeling of social uncertainty that a learner may experience if the target community begins to become a second membership group for him and his ties with his first group begin to loosen in consequence (Lambert, 1963, p. 39; Fishman, 1966b, p. 130). The result may be a feeling of homelessness and sometimes a degree of detachment from both communities similar to what some Anglo-Irish people feel (see p. 80). It is precisely the more advanced and integratively oriented students, says Fishman, who may become embarrassed and alarmed and seek to withdraw from 'the pressures of the direct method' in order to reassert their identity.

Fishman makes it clear that he is not criticizing intensive training by the Direct Method; he merely wants to point out that it 'may require difficult cognitive and emotional adjustments, which may be beyond the limits of some personalities'. Those who succeed in achieving a full command of a second language may have to pay for their flexibility by suffering the pangs of anomie, of rootlessness. But, says Fishman, this is by no means a fatal illness, and he goes on to describe the enrichment that bilingualism can mean to one who has reached a state of balance between his two communities. One may question whether Fishman is correct in saying that anomie is not a fatal illness. Anomie will often lead to anxiety, to mental tension and stress, and tension and stress, as we now know, can kill as surely as other enemies of the body. In the interest of scientific truth a remark should also be added, similar to what Fishman said (see p. 79) about internal American conditions: this state of affairs is man-made; it is not inherent in bilingualism as such. Bilingualism flourishes where the attitude of both communities is favourable and their mutual relations are friendly. We shall briefly consider this subject in the next section.

26 National attitudes

Enough has been said, especially in sections 7 and 10, about the importance for the second-language learner of adopting the right attitude to the target community, of being not only favourably disposed but willing to take on aspects of its behaviour other than purely linguistic ones. What has just been said in section 25 will have made it clear that the target community's attitude to the learner is also not without importance. If the result of successful learning is frowned upon by that community, this will obviously act, if not as a barrier, at least as a discouragement. Similarly, if the source community looks with disfavour upon possible bilingualism among its members, this too will have a deterrent effect. There are indications that attitudes to bilingualism and multilingualism may vary from community to community, some being more favourably disposed than others. Unfortunately such information as we have is fragmentary, often impressionistic and sometimes anecdotal.

Sorensen (1967) mentions an area in the central part of the northwest Amazon where almost every individual is multilingual. A number of tribes live in close proximity in this district; culturally they are homogeneous, and multilingualism is the norm. Each individual will know three, four or more languages, which he will keep carefully apart. Consequently, as Sorensen says, this poses a problem for the generative grammarian, since the ideally fluent speaker–hearer in this part of the world is someone who is *not* unilingual.

In Europe, too, in the Middle Ages and later, an educated person would fairly commonly be able to use one or more languages in addition to his mother tongue. A change came about with the Romantic Movement, at least in western Europe (Forster, 1970). It seems that in Russia until the Revolution many members of the upper class were multilingual. G. W. von Zedlitz (1963, p. 163) tells a story of how in his youth, probably about 1890, he attended a garden party somewhere on the Continent. 'I noticed a tall fine-looking man who spoke English as well as I did; and I at once put him down as an Englishman. Then a few minutes later I heard him speaking French and thought he must, after all, be a Frenchman. But when he began to speak German I *knew* he was a Russian.'

In the course of his work in Montreal (see section 7), Lambert has found that students of French with an integrative motivation generally come from homes where the parents are sympathetically disposed towards French-Canadians. There is no direct link between the students' achievement in French and the parents' knowledge of the language, which need not be very extensive; it is merely the parents' attitude that makes the difference and creates in the students a desire to use French like a Frenchman and to share in the experiences and ways of life and thought of those who speak French. This is not of course directly relevant to what we are discussing in this section, since in this case it is not the whole community but only certain homes that have this attitude; but at least it illustrates the effect of a sympathetic background.

As a contrast one may quote a remark by Robert Graves (1966, p. 49): 'We islanders seldom trust Europeans who speak our own language without a trace of accent or who write it over-well ... I have even known an Englishman to be turned down by the Foreign Service for talking French in too Parisian a style: "Not a reliable type, my dear fellow: obviously suggestible, don't you know"'. A slightly different interpretation of a good knowledge of French is reported by Forster (1970), who says that when his godfather was once heard by a medical colleague to be talking in fluent French to a French visitor, the reaction was, 'Well, Williams, I have always thought that you were a profoundly immoral man, and now I am convinced of it.'

One feeling underlying the Englishman's reaction to the 'too perfect' foreign learner is that of intrusion upon his privacy: it is as if an uninvited guest had started making free with his host's possessions. Moreover, it is felt to be embarrassing not to be able to tell that a man is foreign; one might go and reveal the existence of dirty linen, or one might make remarks about the man's country or about foreigners generally which would be discourteous if one knew he was foreign. There will also, probably, be an instinctive feeling of something which is certainly true, that a member of another nation could not learn to speak like an Englishman without adopting to a large extent an English outlook, linked with a feeling that this is neither proper nor otherwise desirable. Terms such as 'uppish' and 'not to the manner born' reflect aspects of this feeling.

The reaction described here as English is not, in the writer's judgement, either typical or at all common among the other nations within the United Kingdom. This may be because a foreign learner normally models himself on an Englishman, and it would not, obviously, produce the same kind of reaction if a Scot were to mistake a foreigner for a Sassenach. How in fact he would react if he met a foreigner who had acquired a foolproof Scottish form of English it is hard for a non-Scot to say; but probably, on discovering his mistake, he would feel surprised and amused and perhaps even flattered, rather than resentful.

As many have pointed out, there is a striking difference between the English and French attitudes to foreign learners. T. E. Lawrence (1940, p. 355) describes it as follows in reference to the population of the Middle East:

God had not given it them to be English; a duty remained to be good of their type. ... The French, though they started with a similar doctrine of the Frenchman as the perfection of mankind (dogma amongst them, not secret instinct), went on, contrarily, to encourage their subjects to imitate them; since, even if they could never attain the true level, yet their virtue would be greater as they approached it. We looked upon imitation as a parody; they as a compliment.

It is interesting to note that the American approach seems to be in line with the French. Prator (1968, p. 471) says 'The mistrust of French and Americans seems rather to be directed towards the outsider who does *not* speak French or English well.' And he explains the American attitude as due to the experience of absorbing large numbers of immigrants, a circumstance which has created an antipathy to foreign accents. In the Philippines, he says (p. 473), American language policy bore a good deal of resemblance to the French, and he thinks that the explanation is in part 'the American's conviction that his own language – American–English – possesses unequalled virtues, a conviction as unshakable as the similar conviction of the Frenchman.'

An interesting technique developed by Lambert for investigating stereotyped views held by one language group about another consists of asking selected bilingual individuals to read a standard passage first in one language and then in the other. Taped recordings of these readings are afterwards played to groups of judges, who are unaware that they are listening to the same individuals in 'matched guises', and who are asked to evaluate the personality characteristics of each speaker, using 'voice cues' only. The results are often startling (Lambert *et al.*, 1966).

While this technique has no direct relevance to the investigation that we are pursuing here, that of attitudes to learners, Lambert has some interesting speculations about the likely reaction of the judges if they were told that they were listening to the same person in two 'guises'. 'A group of English-Canadian listeners would probably be forced to perk up their ears, reconsider their original classification of the person and then either view him as becoming too intimate in 'their' language or decide otherwise and be pleasantly amazed that one of their own could manage the other group's language so well' (Lambert, 1967, p. 100). Here we meet again our old friend the language-proprietor.

It is worth noting that resentment is not a one-way affair. Foreign learners will often resent the English reaction to 'over-perfection'. Some years ago the present writer threw out the suggestion that an International Standard of English might be created for the use especially of continental nations (Christophersen, 1960). The reaction of Europeans was mostly unfavourable; many rejected indignantly the idea that 'normal' English was to be withheld from them.

The attitudes that we are concerned with here have often been the subject of jokes – for which indeed they are ideally suited – or they have been dismissed as rather trivial affairs causing 'annoying social tugs and pulls' (Lambert, 1967, p. 106). Few who have read that moving document, the autobiography of von Zedlitz, would agree to call them trivial. His share of disappointments in life, rather larger than average it would seem, was not unconnected with his German birth. He was probably never entirely free from 'that instinctive fear that people who were nice and friendly before they knew I had a foreign name, would shrink into their shells when they found out' (1963, p. 84). His English identity, the only fully developed identity that his education had given him, was unacceptable to some people. With cases like this in mind, one wonders a little about the practicality of that 'comfortable bicultural identity' which Lambert (1967, p. 108) holds up as an ideal. Some perhaps achieve it; many do not.

27 National bilingualism

A country undoubtedly derives great advantages from possessing bilingual and bicultural individuals among its citizens (see further p. 93). But this is quite a different situation from that of a bilingual country, which is one that contains more than one mother-tongue group, a situation which is by no means enviable. Some such countries, like Switzerland, achieve harmony and stability; but many do not, because language loyalty will often defeat the wider loyalty. Most such situations have come about through political union of two distinct communities or through large-scale immigration; each language group in these cases is usually conscious of its separate ethnic origin and may resist absorption in a larger unity. In some bilingual countries, like Wales and Ireland, the situation is rather different. Here, despite immigration from England over the centuries, there is no feeling that those who speak English are of different ethnic origin. There is no quarrel between two distinct population groups, each with its own language. There is a problem, nevertheless – namely, whether and how to resist a linguistic flood which has come from outside and has submerged or is threatening to submerge the whole nation.

Historically this situation has of course arisen through the close association of both countries with their more powerful neighbour, England. Free movement of people and the sharing of political and other institutions create a feeling of togetherness, a situation in which the languages become 'alternate' in Wilkins's terminology (section 11), and in which the majority's language will tend to spread, especially if it possesses both prestige and practical advantages. The spread of standard English to Scotland was greatly stimulated by the political union of the countries (Brunner, 1960, p. 178).

Since language teachers produce bilinguals, one may ask.

Could intensive language learning lead to a bilingual situation in a country which is at present unilingual? Prediction in the social sciences is difficult and the following remarks are merely tentative. In the first place, a bilingual situation could obviously only arise if one and the same foreign language occupied a predominant position in all or a majority of a country's schools; secondly, there would need to be a widespread feeling in the country about the usefulness of that foreign language, thus creating an atmosphere favourable to learning and using it; thirdly, freedom of movement between the countries concerned, if not strictly indispensable, would at least greatly assist the process by creating more opportunities to learn and by inducing a feeling of togetherness. In circumstances like these a bilingual situation could arise. This might produce a state of diglossia, of equilibrium between the two languages with each fulfilling a particular role; but there is a considerable risk that the situation might get out of hand; the younger generation might in the end no longer want to learn or use the local language. National bilingualism is sometimes only a transitional stage between two forms of unilingualism.

Five Planning

28 The role of linguistics

This book is something of an exercise in applied linguistics – in the widest sense of that term in which it comprises all systematic knowledge about language in all its aspects. The book has attempted to present information of interest to those who have to plan, or provide for, language learning. In particular it has concentrated on certain neglected or insufficiently explored or understood areas. Is it possible now to draw any conclusions?

It should be emphasized that the role of science, including linguistic science, can never be more than advisory. It can clarify and explain what the various aims involve, and to what extent they are attainable, or mutually compatible, and by what means they might be implemented; but it cannot decide what, if anything, should be done. And it cannot be blamed if some of the information that it provides is unpalatable – if, for instance, the only means by which a particular goal can be reached involves policies which are deemed to be politically undesirable. The nature of language is such that any major decision of policy affects of necessity both the individual and the nation.

29 The individual

The main difficulty on the personal plane derives from the fact that language is linked with personality, with personal identity. This problem of course arises mainly at the advanced level of study; but an integratively oriented course – the most successful type of course – has no easily definable intermediate stages on the way to perfection. The method presupposes willing and active cooperation on the student's part; he is encouraged to adopt an integrative attitude; how, then, can he be told at the same time to hold back a little so as not to become too perfect? This, surely, will largely nullify the beneficial effect of the impetus that an integrative approach confers. It will also, presumably, lose some of the advantages of biculturalism. Some people imagine that one can safely go ahead, since complete success is out of the question anyway; it is hoped that the fallacy of that view will have become clear to readers of chapters 3 and 4.

Warnings have indeed been uttered by various people against 'over-perfection'. Haugen, as quoted by Torrey (1971, p. 252), says, 'To lose one's accent is to identify completely with another society and another way of life. . . . A foreign accent is the foreigner's best passport and the last bastion of his original identity.' Nostrand (1966, p. 4) asks, 'Should one try to be a facsimile of a native – to be really bicultural – or should one try more modestly to be a welcome outsider?' And he feels that the student 'should keep his selfhood undivided and not try to ape another personality'.

It should perhaps be pointed out that 'selfhood' in the above-quoted phrase implies a view that is hardly tenable scientifically. It seems to imply that a person possesses a certain self which he acquired early in life and which will – or should – constitute his personality for ever after, and that any other mode of conduct and way of life that he may learn later will not be really 'his'. But just as a second-learnt language may come to be dominant (see sections 20 and 23), so may – and in most cases will – the accompanying culture. There is nothing in this that is any more strange than cases of social mobility from one walk of life to another. If a garage hand were to become an actor or a director of an engineering works, it would mean that he had developed a somewhat different 'self'. There will be links between his earlier and later selves, but so there will between the two selves in biculturalism.

The important point about this matter is almost certainly, although Nostrand does not expressly say so, that the new 'self' would belong to the culture of another nation; this is probably his reason for using the term 'ape' rather than 'imitate' or 'adopt'. The view that is implied appears to be that to identify oneself to that degree with another nation would not be right and proper, perhaps because nations are felt by many to 'own' their culture in the same way as they 'own' their language. But while the adoption of another 'selfhood' may be accepted by some, and may be rejected by others on ethical or patriotic grounds, or on practical grounds because of the personal difficulties of adjustment and acceptance that it involves, linguistic science can do no more than note these decisions; it cannot lend its weight to any one of them and say it is the right one.

To avoid a clash between two selves, would it be possible to adapt the target language to the source community's culture? For instance, could one have for each foreign country a particular form of English expressing that country's way of life?

In its extreme form this can hardly be said to be a practical solution. If one imagined the source language to be a European language sharing a great deal of vocabulary with English, in the sense that the etymological origin would be the same but the precise meaning and connotation of each word might differ, the result of transferring the foreign meanings and connotations to English would be highly confusing, if at all comprehensible, to one who knew only normal English. Indeed this form of English would probably be useless for most purposes other than simple buying and selling and asking the way to the railway station and other relatively uncomplicated operations like that. The point is that if members of two communities, differing in both language and culture, are to communicate effectively, they have to cross both a language and a culture barrier (see sections 8 and 9). It is probably on the whole easier to cross them in one operation. Certainly the culture barrier must not be forgotten. Even between the most closely related cultures misunderstandings may easily arise, and there can be no short cut to an effective international medium without a fair amount of shared culture. Otherwise most words would have no meaning, or different meanings to different people.

One might imagine a compromise solution, a lightly modified kind of English, a so-called 'limited goal' (Abercrombie, 1956, pp. 37–40), much nearer to normal English than to the learner's culture. There might be relaxation on points where full conformity to general English-speaking practice is not essential, mainly points of pronunciation. The result would be a foreign accent; and it has often been suggested that an accent would be the solution to the problem of the preservation of 'selfhood'. Certainly this would be a way of indicating that the speaker does not belong to the community whose language he is using; but it is often not realized by members of a language community that a foreign speaker with a slight accent has in fact come a very long way culturally as well as linguistically if he is able to achieve fluent and easy communication over a wide range of topics. If he has preserved his 'selfhood' at all, it is only in the sense that he has not – to keep to Haugen's metaphor – surrendered the last bastion of his original identity.

There are two difficulties about this kind of solution. One is that many learners, especially in Europe, object to being debarred from normal English (see p. 85); the result of their efforts may in any case be a foreign accent, but they do not want to aim at this deliberately. The suggestion may have more appeal in some overseas countries, especially where English is a 'second' language in Wilkins's sense, mentioned in section 11. The other objection is that, since the standard would be a synthetic one, there would be no concrete models for the learner to imitate. The learning process would be an essentially different one from that which goes with an integrative approach (Prator, 1968) and hence, presumably, less efficient.

It seems, therefore, that to plan for a deliberate shortfall is difficult if at all possible. Ultimately the individual learner must decide for himself. A warning like Haugen's may suitably be sounded; and at the same time the learner may be reminded of Leopold's idealistic words (1949, p. 188):

I do not overlook the difficulties inherent in growth nourished from a split root instead of a single strong tap root. It will lead to conflicts which can wreck a weak personality, but will improve the mettle of a strong one, which can overcome the difficulties. The difference is the same as between a highly educated and an uneducated person. Ignorance and superstition make the decisions of life simple. Education does not make life easier, but better and richer. Few would condemn education for this reason. Bilingualism should be seen in the same light.

30 The nation

At the national level the problems are largely the same as for the individual learner, but they are of course seen in a different perspective. They centre mostly round the question whether and to what extent the link between political allegiance and linguistic and cultural loyalty can and should be maintained. This link, in large part a product of the nineteenth century, is under some strain nowadays with greatly increased communication between nations, with growing international contacts, formal and informal, over a wide range of activities, and with widening loyalties generally. The nation-state is no longer a self-contained unit. Close cultural relations are an avowed aim of the present age, but that aim implies that some individua's will draw closer in their 'culture', their mode of life, to those of another country. As a result small nations may see their languages threatened. Linguistics can offer no advice beyond pointing out that one cannot 'have it both ways'. Bilingualism, or multilingualism, is probably the best one can hope for.

Several times in our investigation we have come upon the proprietary feeling that some people tend to have in relation to their language. There is no legal or biological basis for such an attitude; it is simply conventional. Where the feeling is strong, it is apt to lead to resentment when others are thought to be appropriating the language and treating it 'as if it were theirs' – 'others' being people who have learnt it as a second language, especially if they belong to another political unit.

This attitude obviously militates against the international use of the language concerned. Since Americans do not possess this feeling, there is reason to expect that American English will make greater headway internationally, as indeed it seems to be doing. The feeling of proprietorship sometimes extends into the sphere of teaching. Some years ago a Middle Eastern country, having failed to recruit teachers of English in Britain, sought them in Germany, where courses were laid on for the teaching of English as a foreign language. Sir David (now Lord) Eccles commented in his capacity as Minister of Education: 'I have nothing against the Germans, but that is our job' (*The Times*, 8 November 1955). Lord Eccles is known to be an advocate of the use of English as a world language, but nothing would be more certain to kill that idea than a British monopoly of the teaching of English.

It has sometimes been pointed out, for instance by Lambert (1967), that a country derives great advantages from possessing bilingual and bicultural citizens. Because of their double allegiance they are less given than others to ethnocentricity; and they can act as links between their two communities. A truly bicultural person is able to 'predict from introspection' (see p. 27) in both his communities; in talking to members of either community he will have a comfortable feeling of understanding what goes on inside their heads; he can strike a common wavelength with them. As we know, many mistakes in foreign policy can be traced to lack of this kind of understanding, to ignorance of foreign psychology. Bilinguals have a great deal to contribute here.

An early example of how bilingualism can smooth over international differences is found in the medieval chronicler Frutolf's account of the setting up of the kingdom of Jerusalem in the first crusade (*Chronicon Universale*, AD 1099, trans. Paul Christophersen). Godfrey of Bouillon, the first ruler of Jerusalem, we are told, 'honoured the soldiers of our [German] race before all other warriors, and commending their fierceness in the most polished manner (*suavissima urbanitate*) to the Gallic knights, managed to allay the natural jealousy which in some way exists between them by his ability to speak both languages like a native (*per innatam sibi utriusque linguae peritiam*).' It is interesting to reflect that many of those who are now building the New Europe possess the same ability as Godfrey of Bouillon.

References

Abercrombie, D. (1956), *Problems and Principles*, Longman.

Alatis, J. E. (ed.) (1970), *Report of the Twenty-First Annual Round-Table Meeting on Linguistics and Language Studies*, Georgetown University Press.

Bateson, P. (1972), 'Naked apes and corporation men', *Listener*, 14 September, pp. 332–5.

Bede (AD 371) *Baedae Opera Historica*, J. E. King (ed.), Loeb Classical Library, 1930.

Bloomfield, L. (1914), *An Introduction to the Study of Language*, Bell & Sons.

Bloomfield, L. (1935), *Language*, Allen & Unwin.

Borst, A. (1957–63), *Der Turmbau von Babel*, vols. 1–4, Anton Hiersemann, Stuttgart.

Braine, M. D. S. (1971), 'The acquisition of language in infant and child', in C. E. Reed (ed.), *The Learning of Language*, Appleton-Century-Crofts.

Brosnahan, L. F. (1960), 'Some aspects of the child's mastery of the sounds in a foster-language', *Studia Linguistica*, vol. 14, pp. 85–94.

Brosnahan, L. F. (1961), *The Sounds of Language*, Heffer.

Brown, R. (1958), *Words and Things*, Free Press.

Brown, T. G. (1969), 'In defense of pattern practice' *Language Learning*, vol. 19, pp. 191–203.

Brunner, K. (1960), *Die englische Sprache*, 2nd edn, vol. 1, Max Niemeyer Verlag, Tübingen.

Carroll, J. B. (1961), *Research on Teaching Foreign Languages*, University of Michigan.

Carroll, J. B. (1963), 'A primer of programmed instruction in foreign-language teaching', *IRAL*, vol. 1, pp. 115–41.

Carroll, J. B. (1966a) 'Research in foreign-language teaching:

the last five years', in R. G. Mead (ed.), *Northeast Conference on the Teaching of Foreign Languages*, Reports of the Working Committees, printed by George Banta Co., Menasha, Wisconsin.

Carroll, J. B. (1966b), 'The contributions of psychological theory and educational research to the teaching of foreign languages', in A. Valdman (ed.), *Trends in Language Teaching*, McGraw-Hill.

Carroll, J. B. (1971a), 'Current issues in psycholinguistics and second-language learning', *TESOL Q.*, vol. 5, pp. 101–14.

Carroll, J. B. (1971b) 'Development of native language skills beyond the early years', in C. E. Reed (ed.), *The Learning of Language*, Appleton-Century-Crofts.

Carthy, J. D. (1966), 'Insect communication', in P. T. Haskell (ed.), *Insect Behaviour*, Royal Entomological Society, London.

Catford, J. C. (1959), 'The teaching of English as a foreign language', in R. Quirk and A. H. Smith (eds.), *The Teaching of English*, Secker & Warburg.

Chomsky, N. (1965), *Aspects of the Theory of Syntax*, MIT Press.

Chomsky, N. (1966), 'Linguistic theory', in R. G. Mead (ed.), *Northeast Conference on the Teaching of Foreign Languages*, Reports of the Working Committees, printed by George Banta Co., Menasha, Wisconsin.

Chomsky, N. (1967), 'The general properties of language', in C. H. Millikan and F. L. Darby (eds.), *Brain Mechanisms Underlying Speech and Language*, Grune & Stratton.

Chomsky, N. (1968), 'Noam Chomsky and Stuart Hampshire discuss the study of language', *Listener*, 30 May, pp. 687–91.

Christophersen, P. (1957), *Some Thoughts on the Study of English as a Foreign Language*, Olaf Norlis Forlag, Oslo.

Christophersen, P. (1960), 'Towards a standard of international English', *English Language Teaching*, vol. 14, pp. 127–38.

Christophersen, P. (1964), 'How do we define our field of study?' in G. I. Duthie (ed.), *English Studies Today*, 3rd series, Edinburgh University Press.

Christophersen, P. (1972), 'Otto Jespersen: a retrospect', *Transactions of the Philological Society*, London.

Colonial Office (1927), *British Tropical Africa: The Place of the Vernacular in Native Education*, Memorandum by the Advisory Committee on Native Education in Tropical Africa, African no. 1110, London.

Dante, *Tutte le Opere di Dante Alighieri*, G. Barbèra (ed.), Florence, 1954.

Darlington, C. D. (1947), 'The genetic component of language', *Heredity*, vol. 1, pp. 269–86.

DeCamp, D. (1969), 'Linguistics and teaching foreign languages', in A. A. Hill (ed.), *Linguistics Today*, Basic Books.

Deutsch, K. W. (1953), *Nationalism and Social Communication*, Wiley.

Diebold, A. R. (1961), 'Incipient bilingualism', *Language*, vol. 37, pp. 97–112.

Dimnet, E. (1935), *My Old World*, Cape.

Elwert, W. T. (1959), *Das zweisprachige Individuum*, Akademie der Wissenschaften und der Litteratur in Mainz, Abhandlungen der geistes- und sozialwissenschaftlichen Klasse, no. 6, Wiesbaden.

Ferguson, C. A. (1959), 'Diglossia', *Word*, vol. 15, pp. 325–40.

Ferguson, C. A. (1971), 'Introduction' to *The Learning of Language*, C. E. Reed (ed.), Appleton-Century-Crofts.

Fishman, J. A. (1966a), *Language Loyalty in the United States*, Mouton.

Fishman, J. A. (1966b), 'The implications of bilingualism for language teaching and language learning', in A. Waldman (ed.), *Trends in Language Teaching*, McGraw-Hill.

Fishman, J. A. (1967), 'Bilingualism with and without diglossia; diglossia with and without bilingualism', *J. soc. Issues*, vol. 23, no. 2, pp. 29–38.

Fishman, J. A. (1968), 'Sociological perspective on the study of bilingualism', *Linguistics*, no. 39, pp. 21–49.

Fishman, J. A. (1970), *Sociolinguistics*, Newbury House, Massachusetts.

Fishman, J. A., Ferguson, C. A. and Das Gupta, J. (eds.) (1968), *Language Problems of Developing Nations*, Wiley.

Forster, L. (1961), 'Fremdsprache und Muttersprache', *Neophilologus*, vol. 45, pp. 177–95.

Forster, L. (1970), *The Poet's Tongues: Multilingualism in Literature*, Cambridge University Press.

Franke, F. (1884), *Die praktische Spracherlernung*, Heilbronn.

Fries, C. C. (1955), 'American linguistics and the teaching of English', *Language Learning*, vol. 6, pp. 1–22.

Frutolf, *Chronicon Universale* (formerly ascribed to Ekkehard of Aura), G. H. Pertz (ed.), *Monumenta Germaniae Historica: Scriptores*, vol. 6, Hanover, 1844.

Gardner, B. T. and Gardner, R. A. (1971), 'Two-way communication with an infant chimpanzee', *Behavior of Nonhuman Primates*, A. M. Schrier and F. Stollnitz (eds.), vol. 4, chapter 3, Academic Press.

Gardner, R. C. (1966), 'Motivational variables in second-language learning', in E. W. Najam (ed.), *Language Learning: The Individual and the Process*, Indiana University Press.

Gladstone, J. R. (1967), 'An experiential approach to the teaching of English as a second language', *English Language Teaching*, vol. 21, pp. 229–34.

Goldstein, K. (1948), *Language and Language Disturbances*, Grune & Stratton.

Graham, R. Somerville (1956), 'Widespread bilingualism and the creative writer', *Word*, vol. 12, pp. 369–81.

Graves, R. (1966), 'Language Levels', *Encounter*, May, pp. 49–51.

Gussman, B. (1960), 'Out in the midday sun', *Listener*, 18 August, pp. 243–4, 278.

Haldane, J. B. S. (1956), 'The argument from animals to men: an examination of its validity for anthropology', *J. roy. anthropol. Inst.*, vol. 86, part 2, pp. 1–14.

Hall, E. T. (1959), *The Silent Language*, quoted from Fawcett Premier edn, 1966, New York.

Hall, R. A. (1964), *Introductory Linguistics*, Chilton Co.

Halliday, M. A. K., McIntosh, A. and Strevens, P. (1964), *The Linguistic Sciences and Language Teaching*, Longman.

Hamilton, E. (1963), *An Irish Childhood*, Chatto & Windus.

Haugen, E. (1955), 'Linguists and the wartime program of language teaching', *mod. language J.*, vol. 39, pp. 243–5.

Haugen, E. (1956), *Bilingualism in the Americas*, Publications of the American Dialect Society, no. 26., University of Alabama Press.

Herodotus, *Herodotus*, A. D. Godley (ed.), vol 1, Loeb Classical Library, 1921.

Higden (1352), in F. Mossé (1952).

Hill, J. H. (1970), 'Foreign accents, language acquisition, and cerebral dominance revisited', *Language Learning*, vol. 20, pp. 237–48.

Hughes, J. P. (1962), *The Science of Language*, Random House.

Hymes, D. H. (1971), 'On communicative competence', quoted from excerpts in J. B. Pride and J. Holmes (eds.), *Sociolinguistics*, Penguin, 1972.

Jakobovits, L. A. (1968), 'Implications of recent psycholinguistic developments for the teaching of a second language', *Language Learning*, vol. 18, pp. 89–109.

Jakobovits, L. A. (1970), *Foreign Language Learning: A Psycholinguistic Analysis of the Issues*, Newbury House, Massachusetts.

Jespersen, O. (1904) *How to Teach a Foreign Language*, Swan Sonnenschein & Co., London.

Jespersen, O. (1922), *Language*, Allen & Unwin.

Jones, W. R. (1960), 'A critical study of bilingualism and non-verbal intelligence', *Brit. J. educ. Psychol*, vol. 30, pp. 71–6.

Joyce, J. (1916), *Portrait of the Artist as a Young Man*, The Egoist.

Kelly, L. G. (ed.) (1969), *Description and Measurement of Bilingualism*, University of Toronto Press.

Kloss, H. (1968), 'Notes concerning a language–nation typology', in J. A. Fishman, C. A. Ferguson and J. Das Gupta (eds.), *Language Problems of Developing Nations*, Wiley.

Kluckhohn, C. and Murray, H. A. (eds.) (1948), *Personality in Nature, Society and Culture*, Knopf.

Krebs, J. P. and Schmaltz, J. H. (1905–7), *Antibarbarus der lateinischen Sprache*, 7th edn, vols. 1–2, Basel.

Kristensen, M. (1926), 'Bidrag til dansk ordhistorie', *Danske Studier*, 1926 vol., pp. 66–76, Copenhagen.

Lado, R. (1964), *Language Teaching: A Scientific Approach*, McGraw-Hill.

Lambert, W. E. (1956), 'Developmental aspects of second-language acquisition', *J. soc. Psychol.*, vol. 43, pp. 83–104.

Lambert, W. E. (1963), 'Psychological approaches to the study of language', *mod. language J.*, vol. 47, quoted from reprint in H. B. Allen (ed.), *Teaching English as a Second Language*, McGraw-Hill, 1965.

Lambert, W. E. (1967), 'A social psychology of bilingualism', *J. soc. Issues*, vol. 23, no. 2, pp. 91–109.

Lambert, W. E., Havelka, J. and Gardner, R. C. (1959), 'Linguistic manifestations of bilingualism', *Amer. J. Psychol.*, vol. 72, pp. 77–82.

Lambert, W. E., Frankel, H. and Tucker, G. R. (1966), 'Judging personality through speech', *J. Communication*, vol. 16, pp. 305–21.

Lambert, W. E., Gardner, R. C., Olton, R. and Tunstall, K. (1968), 'A study of the roles of attitudes and motivation in second-language learning', in J. A. Fishman (ed.), *Readings in the Sociology of Language*, Mouton.

Lamendella, J. T. (1969), 'On the irrelevance of transformational grammar to second-language pedagogy', *Language Learning*, vol. 19, pp. 255–70.

Lawrence, T. E. (1940), *Seven Pillars of Wisdom*, Cape.

Lenneberg, E. H. (1967), *Biological Foundations of Language*, Wiley.

Leonard, S. A. (1962), *The Doctrine of Correctness in English Usage 1700–1800*, Russell & Russell.

Leopold, W. (1949), *Speech Development of a Bilingual Child*, vol. 3, Northwestern University Press.

Levin, H. (1948), *The Essential Joyce*, Cape.

Lyons, J. (ed.) (1970), *New Horizons in Linguistics*, Penguin.

Mackey, W. F. (1966), 'Applied linguistics: its meaning and use', *English Language Teaching*, vol. 20, pp. 197–206.

Macnamara, J. (1966), *Bilingualism and Primary Education*, Edinburgh University Press.

Macnamara, J. (1967). 'The bilingual's linguistic performance', *J. soc. Issues*, vol. 23, no. 2, pp. 58–77.

McNeill, D. (1970), *The Acquisition of Language*, Harper & Row.

Malson, L. (1972), *Wolf Children*, trans. E. Fawcett, P. Ayrton and J. White, New Left Books.

Mencken, H. L. (1941), *The American Language*, 4th edn, Knopf.

Millikan, C. H. and Darley, F. L. (eds.) (1967), *Brain Mechanisms Underlying Speech and Language*, Grune & Stratton.

Morrison, J. R. (1958), 'Bilingualism: some psychological aspects', *The Advancement of Science*, vol. 14, no. 56, pp. 287–90.

Mossé, F. (1952), *A Handbook of Middle English*, trans. J. A. Walker, Johns Hopkins Press.

Newmark, L. (1966), 'How not to interfere with language learning', in E. W. Najam (ed.), *Language Learning: The Individual and the Process*, Indiana University Press.

Newmark, L. and Reibel, D. A. (1968), 'Necessity and sufficiency in language learning', *IRAL*, vol. 6, pp. 145–64.

Nida, E. A. (1958), 'Some psychological problems in second-language learning', *Language Learning*, vol. 8, quoted from reprint in H. B. Allen (ed.), *Teaching English as a Second Language*, McGraw-Hill, 1965.

Nostrand, H. L. (1966), 'Describing and teaching the sociocultural context of a foreign language and literature', in A. Valdman (ed.), *Trends in Language Teaching*, McGraw-Hill.

O'Doherty, E. F. (1958), 'Bilingualism: educational aspects', *The Advancement of Science*, vol. 14, no. 56, pp. 282–7.

Osgood, C. E. and Miron, M.S. (eds.) (1963), *Approaches to the Study of Aphasia*, University of Illinois Press.

Peal, E. and Lambert, W. E. (1962), *The Relation of Bilingualism to Intelligence*, Psychological Monographs: General and Applied, vol. 76, no. 546, American Psychological Association.

Penfield, W. (1958), *The Excitable Cortex in Conscious Man*, Liverpool University Press.

Penfield, W. (1963), *The Second Career*, Little, Brown & Co., Boston and Toronto.

Penfield, W. and Roberts, L. (1959), *Speech and Brain Mechanisms*, Princeton University Press.

Pitscottie, Lindsay of. (c. 1576), *The Historie and Cronicles of Scotland*, vols. 1–3, Æ. J. G. Mackay (ed.), Scottish Text Society, 1899–1911.

Politzer, R. L. (1965), *Foreign Language Learning*, Prentice-Hall.

Prator, C. H. (1964), 'English as a second language: teaching', *Overseas*, vol. 3, quoted from reprint in H. B. Allen (ed.), *Teaching English as a Second Language*, McGraw-Hill, 1965.

Prator, C. H. (1968). 'The British heresy in TESL', in J. A. Fishman, C. A. Ferguson and J. Das Gupta (eds.), *Language Problems of Developing Nations*, Wiley.

Premack, D. (1971), 'On the assessment of language competence in the chimpanzee', in A. M. Schrier and F. Stollnitz (eds.), *Behavior of Nonhuman Primates*, vol. 4, chapter 4, Academic Press.

Pride, J. B. (1971), *The Social Meaning of Language*, Oxford University Press.

Pyles, T. (1971), *The Origins and Development of the English Language*, 2nd edn, Harcourt, Brace Jovanovich.

Rabelais, F. (1532), *Pantagruel*, V. L. Saulnier (ed.), Librairie Droz, Paris, 1946.

Reid, A. (1963), 'Notes on being a foreigner', *Encounter*, June, pp. 28–32.

Richards, I. A. (1967–8), 'Why generative grammar does not help', *English Language Teaching*, vol. 22, pp. 3–9 and 101–6.

Ritchie, W. C. (1967), 'Some implications of generative grammar for the construction of courses in English as a foreign language', *Language Learning*, vol. 17, pp. 45–69, 111–31.

Rivers, W. M. (1964), *The Psychologist and the Foreign-Language Teacher*, University of Chicago Press.

Roddis, M. F. (1968), 'The contemporary relevance of three early works on language-teaching methodology', *IRAL*, vol. 6, pp. 333–47.

Ross, Sir E. Denison (1939), *This English Language*, Longman.

Salimbene de Adam, *Cronica*, G. Scalia (ed.), Bari, 1966.

Sapir, E. (1962), *Culture, Language and Personality*, D. G. Mandelbaum (ed.), University of California Press.

Sapon, S. M. (1965), 'Micro-analysis of second-language learning behaviour', *IRAL*, vol. 3, pp. 131–6.

Singer, M. (1961). 'A Survey of culture and personality theory and research', in B. Kaplan (ed.), *Studying Personality Cross-Culturally*, Harper & Row.

Smith, P. D. (1970), *A Comparison of the Cognitive and Audiolingual Approaches to Foreign Language Instruction*, Center for Curriculum Development, Philadelphia.

Soffietti, J. P. (1955), 'Bilingualism and biculturalism', *J. educ. Psychol.*, vol. 46, pp. 222–7.

Sorensen, A. P. (1967), 'Multilingualism in the northwest Amazon', *Amer. Anthropol.* vol. 69; a revised version is printed in J. B. Pride and J. Holmes (ed.), *Sociolinguistics*, Penguin, 1972.

Spitzer, L. (1948), *Essays in Historical Semantics*, S. F. Vanni, New York.

Sweet, H. (1877), *A Handbook of Phonetics*, Clarendon Press.

Sweet, H. (1899), *The Practical Study of Languages*, Dent.

Tillotson, G. (1959), Review of R. Fréchet's *George Borrow*, *Modern Language Review*, vol. 54, pp. 266–7.

Torrey, J. W. (1971), 'Second-language learning', in C. E. Reed (ed.), *The Learning of Language*, Appleton-Century-Crofts.

Trevisa, John of (1385), in F. Mossé (1952).

Viëtor, W. (1882), *Der Sprachunterricht muss umkehren*, published under the pseudonym 'Quousque Tandem', Leipzig.

Wain, J. (1961), 'A visit to India', *Encounter*, May, pp. 3–15.

Weinreich, U. (1953), *Languages in Contact*, Publications of the Linguistic Circle of New York, no. 1.

Weisgerber, L. (1938), 'Ist *muttersprache* eine germanische oder eine romanische wortprägung?', *Beiträge zur Geschichte der deutschen Sprache und Litteratur*, vol. 62, pp. 428–37.

Wilkins, D. A. (1972), *Linguistics in Language Teaching*, Arnold.

Wooldridge, D. E. (1963), *The Machinery of the Brain*, McGraw-Hill.

Zedlitz, G. W. von (1963), *The Search for a Country*, Paul's Book Arcade, Wellington, New Zealand.

Index